✧Constitutional Revolution✧

CONSTITUTIONAL REVOLUTION

The Link between Constitutionalism and Progress

✦ ✦ ✦

Ulrich K. Preuss

Translated by
Deborah Lucas Schneider

HUMANITIES PRESS
NEW JERSEY

Originally published as *Revolution, Fortschritt und Verfassung* in 1990 by Verlag Klaus Wagenbach GmbH.

English translation first published 1995 by Humanities Press International, Inc., Atlantic Highlands, New Jersey 07716.

English translation © 1995 by Humanities Press International, Inc.

Library of Congress Cataloging-in-Publication Data
Preuss, Ulrich Klaus, 1939–
    [Revolution, Fortschritt und Verfassung. English]
    Constitutional revolution: the link between constitutionalism and progress / Ulrich K. Preuss ; translated by Deborah Lucas Schneider.
      p.   cm.
    Includes index.
    ISBN 0–391–03853–2.—ISBN 0–391–03854–0 (pbk.)
    1. Representative government and representation—History.
    2. Revolutions—History. I. Title.
    JF1051.P7213 1995
    323'.042—dc20   94–37939
                                             CIP

A catalog record for this book is available from the British Library.

Printed in the United States of America

✧Contents✧

✧ Introduction ✧

Constitution-Making and the Foundation of a New Polity

I

This book does not deal with constitutionalism, or at best it does so only marginally, although it is full of talk about constitutions. It is a book about the *meaning* which constitutions and constitution-making have had in different societies and in exceptional times. That we have lived in exceptional times since 1989 is beyond question. In the years 1989–1993 the political map of Europe has been changed more profoundly than in the preceding seventy years, with seemingly eternal and powerful states breaking apart and vanishing while new states emerge. Perhaps Poles know best about this. They talk to the West European visitor with a mixture of pride about their own political coherence and continuity as a state, and amazement about the rapidity with which the basic circumstances of their foreign policy have changed. Between 1989 and 1993, their country acquired a completely new set and number of neighbors: Instead of the three former states, the Soviet Union, Czechoslovakia, and the GDR, there is now a bundle of no less than seven, reaching from a small part of Russia (the exclave around Kaliningrad) over Lithuania, Belorussia, Ukraine, Slovakia, and the Czech Republic to the (enlarged) Federal Republic of Germany. This is only the most apparent manifestation of a new Great Transformation which Europe has undergone and which is still underway.

This transformation is by no means restricted to Eastern and central Europe. By a historical coincidence, both Western and Eastern Europe are going through a phase of political reconstruction. With the Treaty on European Union (the Maastricht treaty), the member states of the European Community (EC) are on their way to a political union which is envisioned as leading to the birth of a supranational European state. However remote this future may be, in EC-Europe the heyday of the European national state seems to have passed, while the postcommunist states of Eastern and southeastern Europe

1

are taking the opposite course. Having been forced to commit themselves more or less hypocritically to the ideal of internationalism on behalf of the universalist moral of communism for more than forty years, the idea of the homogeneous nation-state has now become the most powerful paradigm of self-definition in both their domestic and international politics. Paradoxically, these simultaneous and dissimilar developments in Eastern and Western Europe are even tied together in that some of the postcommunist countries — Hungary, the Czech Republic, Slovakia, and Poland — are making every effort to become members of the EC as soon as possible. Since this implies taking part in the ongoing process of continual political integration, this policy may amount to the seemingly oxymoronic situation of revitalizing national statehood and diffusing it at the same time.

While I pass over the matter of which of the two discrepant tendencies is more up-to-date and more in line with the necessities and requirements of what has become our "global village," I want to deal with the role which constitutions play in this process. Evidently, we are experiencing an era of rampant political founding. This has far-reaching consequences on the structure of the international order and international politics. But it also gives rise to the question of whether the political founders will dispose of the techniques which seem indispensable for the creation of a durable, viable, and civilized polity. It is the question about the role of constitutions and of constitution-making in the making of a new political world in Europe.

II

In the past two hundred years constitutions have been the most visible and most symbolic manifestation of a people's determination to establish an entirely new basis of its polity. The French Revolution was initiated when the Third Estate declared itself as the constituent assembly of the French nation, and all major political changes that followed became subject to the sanction of, or even the sanctification by, a new constitution. Not accidentally, in the last two hundred years France has experienced no fewer than twelve constitutions, and to a certain degree this relation between democratic revolutions and constitutions has been the predominant pattern of almost all continental European countries. According to this pattern, constitutions anoint successful democratic revolutions in that they solemnly confirm that through its revolutionary actions the people has regained its constituent power, that is, a power unrestricted by rules, institutions, or superior orders and directed only by its unrestrained willpower. The incarnation of this will is the constitution.[1]

The inherent connection between the revolutionary will of the people and

the making of a constitution may explain the urgent quest and the unremit-
ting enthusiasm for a new constitution which is one of the distinctive fea-
tures of the French Revolution, the mother of all modern revolutions, as it
were. As will be shown in the following chapters in greater detail, at the
very beginning of the constitutional epoch in Europe the ideas of revolution, popular sovereignty, political and social progress, and constitutionalism were closely associated with each other in that they mutually supported
and even explained one another. The French revolutionaries envisioned the
constitution, which they viewed as originating in the constituent power of
the autonomous and supreme will of the nation, as the untainted expression
of the revolutionary spirit of the people—and clearly this spirit was imbued
with the desperate quest for liberation from the miseries of their lives.

Although we are again living through an era of constitution-making, the
hopes which both the masses and the elites associate with this undertaking
are evidently considerably lower. Indeed, in the years since 1989 the European continent has undergone social and political changes which are hardly
less radical and far-reaching than those in the last quarter of the eighteenth
century. Likewise, we can assume that the reshaping of the political, economic, and social structures of the Eastern European countries which have
overturned communist rule has the unequivocal meaning that the new elites
are engaging in a process of constitution-making. However, it is far from
clear whether the peoples of these countries are ready to invest their trust in
a better future in the intelligent construction of a new constitution. After the
high-spirits of the first months following the overturn of the old regimes,
the main concern of both the ordinary people and the new political elites
has been the satisfaction of the basic economic needs of the populace, and
it is not at all obvious that, after all, constitutions really do make a difference.

So, first of all, what does it mean to create a constitution for a polity? In
premodern times empires and polities were founded by spiritual, military, or
political leaders. Their work became an integral part of a cosmos which
embodied the existing religious, epistemological, and political order. Normally these foundations played a pivotal role in the myths and narratives
which transmuted them into sacred events in a history of salvation. Each
individual was unquestionably supposed to have an innate knowledge and
understanding of the duties which followed from his or her being part of
this suprapersonal and spiritual order.

There was nothing like a choice between different institutional devices
and strategies, because the foundation of a polity was not a rational and
planned venture performed according to a blueprint but an event which gradually adopted the character of a founding act only in the tales of succeeding

generations. Moreover, the foundation of a polity was a purely de facto event which acquired legal significance at best in subsequent historical development in which physical domination was transformed step-by-step into institutionalized authority. In contrast, constitution-making is a deliberate act of political foundation which not only aims at the creation of a legal order but which is itself already a legal act — the exercise of the constituent power.[2] Being directed at the creation of an order whose structure is, so to speak, anticipated in its actions, the constituent power ceases to be mere force. This simultaneity of facticity and validity[3] may explain why the constituent power has always been somewhat mysterious, ever since its first construction in the age of the liberal revolutions of the last quarter of the eighteenth century.

The idea that the foundation of a polity was the deliberate act of a constituent power could not arise before the understanding began to spread in the seventeenth century that the social order was a work of man and especially that political rule had to be grounded on the consent of the ruled. There were already constitutional elements in the European legal tradition long before the triumph of the concepts of rational natural law, social contract, and finally constitutionalism.[4] Not accidentally, the etymology of the terms "citizen" and "citoyen," and of the German term "Bürger," as well, is rooted in the medieval free towns, because long before the beginning of the modern state they had already developed a rather modern political structure, in particular independence from the church and initial steps toward political representation. But this kind of representation was still based on the concept of social estates. Thus, in order to become a forceful idea that was able to change radically the perception of political power and to claim universal recognition and fulfillment, a thoroughly modern concept of the individual had to emerge: first, the idea of individual equality and second, the picture of an individual whose trust in the eternal persistence of institutions, which conveyed security against the frightening horrors of the world, had worn away. The world had to be reconstructed from the beginning, and in order to develop a sense of security and trust the individuals had to become the founders of their institutions all by themselves and by rational design. The political order became subject to secular justifications according to the standards of reason.

III

Our own theoretical narrative tells us that this reason leads the individuals to conclude two different contracts, namely, first, the contract of association, which allows them to leave the "state of nature" and to establish a society in the first place, and second, the contract of domination, which stipulated the right to rule and the duty to obey.[5] While the former is a contract between all individuals who want to enter into the state of civility, the latter is a contract between the rulers and the ruled; it is a contract in which the people promise obedience to the ruler, who in turn guarantees their security and the enjoyment of their rights. It is this contract of domination which creates a polity. It lays the philosophical foundation of what later evolves to the constitution in the strict sense of the word. It defines the modern standard of political foundation, negatively in that it rejects both religious or other kinds of spiritual revelation and pure military force as rightful bases for a polity, and positively in that it commands that political rule must be justified through the interest or the will of the ruled. From now on, even the hereditary monarchy is no longer established by God's mercy but is justifiable only by the monarch's obligation to pursue the common good, the public welfare, the public interest, or whatever terms have been and are still being used for the purely immanent and secular character of modern political rule.

At the latest since the French Revolution, the standard by which the civilized character of a political regime has been gauged is its quality as a power which has been framed, that is, which has gained independence from the arbitrariness and capricious subjectivity of the ruler or a ruling elite. This is the most elementary meaning of constitutional rule. A regime which does not meet this standard is simply out of date; it may endure for a time, perhaps even a fairly long time, but since it lacks legitimacy and is erected on pure power, it degenerates to despotism. Hence, constitutional rule has a significance which transcends the prima facie meaning of limited government in the sense that it was defined in the famous Article 16 of the Declaration of the Rights of Man and of the Citizen, namely, as essentially including the separation of powers and the guarantee of a bill of rights. Although indeed this *limiting* function of the constitution is of utmost importance, it is obvious that nobody can found a polity on the basis of the principle of limited government without having constituted and legitimized the power of the polity in the first place. Hence, the order is reversed: to found or restructure a polity requires, first and foremost, the *creation* of its very power (which one might call the creative or constitutive force of the constitution); second, the constitution's force to *legitimize* political domination; and third, its function as an *integrative* means of transforming a multitude of individuals into one people, that is, into a political body. Not coincidentally, the concept of the nation, one of the most powerful political ideas of the nineteenth century, appeared at almost the same time as the idea of constitutionalism, and no less coincidentally Emmanuel-Joseph Sieyès connected them with each other by defining the nation in constitutional terms. According to his definition, a nation is "a body of associates living under common laws and represented by the same legislative assembly."[6] Last, but not least, there is the limiting function of the constitution already referred to.

IV

For the individual to live under a constitution means not to be a mere object of domination but to be recognized as a person vested with rights, to live in a nation, to be a member, that is, a citizen of this nation, not to be alienated from his or her fellowman and from the community into which he or she is born, to enjoy equal civil rights and liberties, to be represented in the legislative body of this nation, and last but not least, to be part of the persistent collective undertaking to civilize political power and to ban violence from shaping the polity.

Hence to make a constitution does not just mean to change the mode of domination. It is tantamount to the creation of a new universe. Throughout the millenia this was a divine domain, even if God did employ the help of outstanding human beings like Moses or Saint Peter in order to perform his sacred work. This is why from the very beginning of the era of constitution-making this undertaking, though thoroughly secular, has always been regarded as a quasi-sacred task which could only be performed by somebody who equalled God and his omnipotence in the secular sphere: the people. But constitution-making entailed a special difficulty which neither God nor the absolutist princes of past ages had to meet and whose mastery demanded unprecedented capabilities. God did not create the order of the world for himself but for mankind; the sovereign princes and monarchs of the past unilaterally imposed their rule on their subjects without being themselves subjects to it. In contrast, constitution-making necessarily means that the authors of their creation are simultaneously their subjects. For the first time in the history of human reasoning about a good and just order two conditions applied simultaneously: First, its creators were omnipotent—that is, they were not bound by the rules and dictates of a preexisting order—and second, the rules and institutions which they created applied to themselves. This exceptional situation may have produced horror rather than delight, for, although these creators are, like God, omnipotent in the secular sphere, they are, unlike him, fallible. Their work is likely to fall victim to their unavoidable human sinfulness and weakness.

Jean-Jacques Rousseau himself, who was the first to pronounce the people's secular omnipotence, shrank from the consequences of his doctrine and demanded the godlike person of a lawgiver. In order to find the appropriate rules of peaceful and fruitful social cooperation,

> there would need to exist a superior intelligence, who could understand the passions of men without feeling any of them, who had no affinity with our nature but knew it to the full, whose happiness was independent of ours, but who would nevertheless make our happiness his concern, who would be content to wait in the fullness of time for a distant glory, and to labour in one age to enjoy the fruits in another. Gods would be needed to give men laws.[7]

Constitution-making, however, is of course not a suprahuman venture. It must and can only be accomplished by humans, and thus it is necessarily vulnerable to their limited intelligence, their passions, their weaknesses of will, and their incapacity "to labour in one age to enjoy the fruits in another." In fact, constitution-making is an undertaking just as uncertain and risky as any other human activity, but while other human activities are confined and checked by their embeddedness in a broad variety of social relations and shaped by manifold institutions, constitution-making is vested with supreme and unrestrained power. This describes the exceptional character of constitution-making: It is a divine end which has to be accomplished with human means. Therefore constitution-making does not just mean wielding power and enjoying the omnipotence of a secular God; it involves the risk of potential failure and self-inflicted misery. This makes constitution-making a reflexive human undertaking. The meaning of reflexivity and its implications in the area of constitutionalism will be explicated in the last chapter. What has to be underscored here is that to take part in the rare venture of constitution-making is not just an exciting and demanding venture, but it also requires a particular kind of knowledge, intelligence, and wisdom, namely, the awareness of the unbridgeable discrepancy between a people's power to erect a polity and its intellectual and moral abilities to satisfy the responsibilities which this unlimited power involves.

V

It should be mentioned that the electrifying sensation which participation in constitution-making may release is not necessarily the privilege of a previous founding generation. Nor does it require a completely new constitution during the lifespan of every generation. If this were so, the American people would have to be pitied for the longevity of their constitution, and the French would merit our envy for having had the chance to create twelve constitutions in less than two hundred years. Whether this is really so need not be decided here. Rather, it is important to point to the possibility that profound political changes, even a sweeping reconstitution of the polity, may take place within the framework of an already existing constitution. Bruce Ackerman has claimed that in the American case there was not only the act of foundation — the creation of the American Constitution *senso strictu* — but the eras of Reconstruction (with the post–Civil War amendments) and the New Deal, events which he, in contrast to the prevailing professional narrative of American constitutional lawyers, views as no less creative than the creation of the Constitution itself.[8]

This interesting interpretation of the constitutional history of the United States enriches our understanding of constitutionalism altogether. It suggests the possibility of a revolution within the framework and on the basis of an existing constitution. I do not intend to go into closer scrutiny of Ackerman's contention; rather, I want to hint at the potentiality of the reverse case, namely, the profound change, in fact, the abolishment of the essential elements of an economic and political order, including its constitutional protection, in an unambiguously non- and even antirevolutionary spirit which remains firmly loyal to the basic principles of constitutionalism. This is how the processes in Eastern and central Europe might be interpreted. As will be demonstrated in chapter 5, the elimination of the communist regimes and the erection of profoundly new economic, social, and political structures happened, with few exceptions, within the framework of the existing constitution of the respective country. Before the revolutionaries overturned the old regimes, they amended the communist constitutions according to the amending procedures of those very constitutions. Thus, for example, the leading role of the Communist Party, which in fact meant the dictatorship of the *nomenklatura*, or the category of the people's property were not abolished until the pertinent articles of the constitution had been repealed. Having been forced to listen to hypocritical revolutionary phraseology and having experienced an all-pervasive legal nihilism for the preceding forty years, the anticommunist opposition wanted to be neither revolutionary nor negligent of the rule of law. Thus it is not at all surprising that many of them plainly deny the revolutionary character of the downfall of the old regimes. They prefer to interpret it as an act of resistance against a lawless regime.

Of course, the distinction between *revolution* and *resistance* has serious implications. It means, among other things, that the erection of new constitutional structures, in fact, of a thoroughly new polity, is less a creative and founding act of a new beginning than a *restitutive* activity of restoring the integrity of a rule of law which preexists and which never ceased to exist beneath the surface of an inherently lawless regime imposed by mere force. In this context the two meanings of the priority of the rule of law are frequently blurred: It may refer either to the chronological antecedence of the rule of law in the historical phase of the precommunist era of the respective country or to the superior character of the philosophical ideas of natural law in the hierarchy of political and legal concepts. Depending on which understanding prevails, the invocation of the principle of rule of law either means simple restoration of a previous order (whereby the restitution is regarded as a redress of previous injustice required by the rule of law), or it entails the categorical imperative not only to establish an order in which the rule of law is the paramount principle but also to carry out the transition from the communist regime to the rule-of-law principle itself according to the dictates of the rule of law.[9] Unlike the understanding of rule of law as an order of restitution, in the latter case the principle of rule of law does not look into the past but into the future. Still, it excludes the idea of a sovereign lawmaking power. Although in the postcommunist countries the old constitutions are thoroughly amended or completely new constitutions are created, the idea of constitution-making in the revolutionary sense elaborated above is implicitly or explicitly rejected. The revolutionaries of 1989 do not want to be godlike and to assume the burden of a completely new beginning with all its demanding requirements. This is fully understandable. Moreover, many of those who receive such a request rightly object that there is no necessity to reinvent the wheel—all relevant constitutional ideas and institutions have been invented in the past two hundred years. Why not rely on the accumulated wisdom of this constitutional history?

VI

However, four years of experience with the political and economic outcomes of the economic and political transformations of 1989 raises the question whether part of the serious problem actually confronting most of the postcommunist countries of Eastern and central Europe are due to neglecting the far-reaching significance of the "constitutional question."

This is particularly true with regard to the interdependence of the economic and the politico-institutional issues. It is especially the role of private property, both in the economic and in the political sphere, which still appears to be less than clear. The complexity of this question has only evolved gradually. At the very outset the relations between economic and constitutional transformation looked rather simple. At first glance, the Eastern and central European revolutions of 1989 seemed to have the merely negative implication of delegitimizing the old power elites and of devaluating their usurped authority and command over the whole economy. Consequently, nothing more seemed to be required for the realization of the goals of the revolution than the reestablishment of private property and the freedom of contract. It has widely been believed that the mere actuality of these two essential legal institutions would inevitably cause the spontaneous emergence of a market economy. After all, the French Revolution abolished feudal domination and its incident privileges, immunities, and powers, replaced them with the rights to freedom and property, and achieved a market economy. Why should the antisocialist revolutions be different? They, too, aim at the abolition of an unproductive class and its obnoxious rule, and what they need is no more than what the French accomplished, namely, the creation of a constitution which included the core institutions of private autonomy and private property.

But the analogy is questionable. We have to take into account two major differences. First, in eighteenth-century France the Third Estate did already exist prior to the Revolution, and it had already emerged as a class which dominated those parts of the economy which had become subject to marketization. Their revolutionary struggle aimed at a constitutional framework which protected their entrenched interests as an already existing socioeconomic class. Since their industry, diligence, skills, and achievements had been frustrated by the *ancien régime* time and again, property was the institution which could provide the unthwarted enjoyment of the fruits of their achievements. In other words, the institution of private property did not serve as a midwife for the creation of a new class of capitalist entrepreneurs but referred to an already existing propertied class.

Evidently, the situation in the postcommunist societies is the reverse. Private property is intended to generate the very interests, skills, and entrepreneurial attitudes and ultimately the social class which develops these characteristics, so that private property would serve less the purpose of protecting a preexisting class than of developing it in the first place. This, then, raises the serious question of how to find a justifiable method of assigning first property rights.[10] Ironically, the situation has some similarity with the Bolshevik Revolution, which also created the institutional framework for the rule of the proletariat which was expected to come to light as a consequence of this very revolution.

The second dissimilarity between the French Revolution and the Great

Transformation of 1989 refers to what one may call the different prepolitical, mostly cultural perceptions of private property. In the French Revolution, private property protected the wealth-engendering capacity of the emerging capitalist class. It did not necessarily protect their accumulated assets; these remained exposed to the uncertainties of the market, which conveyed great risks and great opportunities as well. With the call for noninterference by the state in the market process, the liberals of the eighteenth century did not mean to demand protection of their assets but the autonomous operation of a sphere which promised enormous economic gains. The insecurity of the market was balanced by its opportunities. Similarly, when they claimed the sanctity of property, they did not have in mind physical things in the first place. What was vital about property was the legal institution, that is, the power to make any kind of transaction with one's acquisitions without being bound by considerations about other individuals' needs. An important element of the meaning of property was the emancipation of a person's assets from social duties. Henceforth the sanctity of property was defined as the owners' power to exclude each and everybody from taking, using, or affecting the individuals' land and other things which they had appropriated through their work, their skills, and their relentless struggle with the hardships of their lives. No less important was the meaning which followed from the quality of property as a *legal institution*, namely, the guarantee of the security of a person's possessions. The security of property permitted long-term calculations and provided a framework of predictability and reliability for investments. Here, too, property served as an incentive for entrepreneurial and risk-taking activities. This quasi-creative function of property led some of the forefathers of bourgeois liberalism to esteem property even more highly than life and liberty, because the guarantee of security was regarded as the hallmark of civilization which symbolized the triumph over the state of nature.[11]

Evidently, the constitutional protection of property in the postcommunist countries cannot have the same function as it did after the French Revolution. As I already mentioned, neither is there an entrepreneurial class for which the protection of property serves less the safe possession of wealth than the calculability of possibly daring economic transactions and profitable investments, nor is property today an institution whose positive contribution to the weal of a society lies in its social exclusivity.

If it holds true that, unlike after the French Revolution, this time merely removing the main political and economic elements of the old regime will not create a passable market economy, then the postcommunist countries cannot escape the task of conceiving constitutions which go beyond this negative approach and aspire to positively devise a new political order. If they face up to this challenging undertaking, they will soon recognize that property is a necessary but not a sufficient condition for the solution of the urgent problems of their poorly functioning economies. True, in all modern societies in which large segments of the populace enjoy a high standard of living some private property is constitutionally protected. But the reverse statement does not apply: Not all countries that protect the institution of private property can provide a high standard of living for the majority of their populace. Hence it would be incorrect to equate a full-fledged market economy including private property with an average high standard of living found in the industrialized West and Japan; private property is the symbol of an entrepreneurial and potentially dynamic economy, but it is not the shibboleth for mass welfare.

To devise a constitution in which the guarantee of private property is not just the symbol of hope for mass welfare, it is necessary to understand the complex social, political, and cultural preconditions of private property. Undoubtedly the right to private property includes the legal protection of the possession of physical things. But its main relevance lies in its *relational character*, that is, in its embeddedness in a complex infrastructure which includes systems of transportation, communication, financial services, legal regulations of technical norms and quality standards, of industrial relations, environmental protection, the internal structure and external relations of companies, economic competition, and much more. Modern private property is not wealth generating by itself, but only when it is well adjusted and responsive to an ever-changing social environment which exposes it to the pressure to generate the necessary returns for reinvestment in order to escape the prospect of devaluation. To be sure, these conditions can and do vary considerably, as a rough comparison between the market economies of, say, Sweden, the United States, and South Korea patently displays. To a considerable extent, these variations are due to conditions which depend on the political structure of the respective countries or which are subject to political decisions. In other words, they are mostly due to the sphere of politics.

Nowhere did the social framework of private property emerge spontaneously through an invisible hand. In the Western democracies they were *gradually developed* in frequently arduous, sometimes violent struggles within the framework and with the creative use of the institutional devices of mass democracy; in other countries, as in South Korea, they have been *imposed* through an authoritarian regime which identified itself with the imperatives of a rigid capitalist market economy (which does not necessarily imply competitive markets). This authoritatively planned and imposed capitalism obviously has other characteristics than does the capitalism which originated from revolutions which realized individual freedom and successively paved the way for democratic rule. The striking feature of the Eastern European transformations of 1989 is what one may understand as the call for a *self-imposed* capitalism, that is, a capitalism which is neither imposed by a nondemocratic authoritarian regime nor gradually developed in democratic struggles but authoritatively imposed by the will and the fiat of the demos itself.

VII

This has implications which may not have been fully anticipated by the proponents of this program and which may have thorny consequences for the constitutional development of the respective countries. Taken at face value, it implies the willingness of the people to submit themselves to the inherent imperatives of an economic order as it is defined by those actors who are its immediate beneficiaries and who in all likelihood are predominantly committed to the goal of quick and unscrupulous self-enrichment or, at best, to a regime of uncompromising economic efficiency. The constitutional framework that would most probably fit into this socioeconomic and sociopolitical scheme would be an authoritarian democracy, which in all likelihood will restrict the right of the people to revoke or to qualify their commitment to a capitalist market economy and which will probably depoliticize the emerging texture of civil society and establish a strong presidency at the expense of parliamentary power. In this perspective, the preference for presidential systems which we can observe in many of the postcommunist countries appears to be less the heritage of communism than a structural consequence of the choice for a self-imposed capitalism. Since regimes of both imposed and self-imposed capitalism tend to neglect the complex relational character of private property and of its entanglement with the texture of a differentiated democratic society, they are particularly vulnerable to the danger of authoritarianism. The interrelation between the free-market option and the authoritarian potential of a presidential form of government is particularly revealing in the case of Russia in the spring of 1993: The popularly elected president had become the only remaining safeguard for the introduction of a market economy which is more laissez-faire-like than the market economies in any one of the capitalist countries which the new elites regarded as a model. Sometimes this type of authoritatively self-imposed capitalism and democracy produces caricaturist effects. So it was reported that after the accident in the nuclear plant of Tomsk in April

1993, Russian president Boris Yeltsin ordered the mass media to report truthfully about this accident and its consequences and about future accidents. Obviously this is the modern version of Rousseau's famous paradox that some people must be forced to be free; in this case the Russian people forced themselves to be free.

Why should the people be ready to submit themselves to the extreme uncertainties and, for most of them, hardships of an authoritarian capitalism? It is not very probable that they have a long-term conception of their society's development which persuades them to voluntarily endure the misery of the present for the sake of future benefits which may only materialize in the next generation. In order to form a more realistic hypothesis, we should come back to an observation which I made above: the assumption of the postrevolutionary governments in Eastern and central Europe (including the government of Germany with regard to its economic policies vis-à-vis the former GDR) that the market is a spontaneous order which autonomously and automatically generates efficiency, productivity, and wealth once all obstacles to its unimpeded operation have been abolished. More or less explicitly it is taken for granted that all that is necessary is the eradication of the characteristics of the old regime: state property, state planning, state bureaucracy, and state power to make all relevant decisions about investment, prices, consumption, the allocation of resources, and so on. The market is supposed to be suffocated by a command economy, and therefore it is ready to reemerge once the barriers that prevented it from its autonomous operation are removed.

Evidently, this is an erroneous presumption. As I already stated, the market economies in the Western European countries originated from relentless and violent social struggles which lasted several generations. Moreover, except for a rather short period of laissez-faire capitalism in some countries, the market economy, once established, has always been subject to more or less intense political regulation. The market is not a spontaneous and autonomously functioning order, nor can it be built ex nihilo, this "nihil" being freedom in the negative sense: the absence of obstacles to one's actions. The prevailing understanding of the postcommunist elites seems to be that they (or, for that matter, those who pushed forward the development in 1989) created this "nihil," which then became the starting point for the spontaneous emergence of a new socioeconomic order. More or less consciously it is assumed that there is one single starting point for the release of an autonomous economic development into a better future.

In this frame of understanding the revolutionary call for a market economy can be understood as an integral part of the negative program of the revolution. It is a concomitance of the abolishment of the communist regime and of its pervasive interference with the people's personal lives. On account of the complex preconditions of a market economy, it is in fact a positive program for the future order of society and, moreover, a rather demanding one. What is even more amazing is the presumption that the market is less a problem-solving institution than the solution of all economic problems, the only qualification being that the people are required to summon some patience before its beneficent effects will materialize. If this hypothesis can claim some plausibility, it could help to explain the paradox of the people's call for a self-imposed capitalism. Moreover, it would reveal that the idea of progress which played a pivotal role — at least in the continental European variant of constitutionalism — has almost completely lost its moral connotations.

If this concept still plays any role at all, it is diffused in the anonymous operation of a market economy. But while at the end of the eighteenth century it was the force of the moral argument which demanded the freedom and self-determination of the individual and which finally unbound the — morally less attractive — forces of the market, at the end of the twentieth century the causal link between these two intimately connected elements seems to have been reversed in the minds of many protagonists of the postcommunist countries in Eastern Europe: Once the forces of economic activity have been released, progress in all other spheres of life, including the moral life, will necessarily develop. Ironically, this assumption was also one of the basic beliefs of the Marxist theory. This, of course, does not mean that in the postcommunist countries there is still a hidden Marxism at work. Rather, it demonstrates what has been observed many times, namely, that liberalism and Marxism, although hostile to each other in many respects, share some essential theoretical postulates. At least a radical liberalism à la Hayek (which plays a major role in the thinking of many reformers in Eastern Europe) displays a striking similarity with Marxist tenets. One of them is the belief that the autonomous operation of anonymous social forces — be it the invisible hand of the market or the contradiction between the productive forces and the organization of the means of production — is the great mover of society, which therefore is largely unamenable to deliberate acts of self-organization and self-improvement. But it is exactly this presumption which feeds the idea of constitutionalism.

VIII

This leads back to the question of whether and how constitutions can contribute to the well-being of a polity in general and to the transformation of a Communist Party dictatorship into a durable democratic system in particular. It is striking feature of many debates about constitutionalism and its role in the political life of a society that reference is made to some preconstitutional potential which is supposed to be the true moving force behind the web of constitutional and legal rules. As I stated above, in the economic sphere the invisible hand of the market ("the market forces") is the best-known candidate for this presupposition. In the sphere of politics we can frequently find very similar ideas. I refer to the widely held view that it is the primary, perhaps even the sole function of constitutions to restrict and to check a preexisting sphere of the political,[12] which is presumed to embody simultaneously both the genuinely creative potential of the modern polity and its dangerous and unfathomable abyss: the people. This is of course not surprising in a tradition in which "We the people . . . establish this Constitution," or in which the principle of popular sovereignty is laid down as the genuine foundation of the polity (as in the French tradition). What is worth emphasizing here is the widely held presumption of a certain tension, perhaps even hostility, between the people and the constitution. In this respect even the proponents of the most antagonistic concepts of constitutionalism, namely, Rousseau on the one hand and the Federalists on the other, concurred, although of course they drew radically different conclusions from this assumption. For Rousseau the will of the people is the ultimate source of any kind of political authority; to bind it is tantamount to degrading the people into the status of slaves. The popular will is the supreme law of the land, and no source of knowledge, wisdom, justice, or equity other than the people can claim to come up to, much less to surpass, it in this political capacity. To subject the people to any kind of constraint, be it imposed or self-imposed, meant to destroy it. "If a people promises simply and solely to obey, it dissolves itself by that very pledge; it ceases to be a people; for once there is a master, there is no longer a sovereign, and the body politic is therefore annihilated."[13]

This was of course the opposite of what the Federalists strongly believed, but they, too, were fully convinced that there is an inherent tension between the people and the constitution. While Rousseau wanted to protect the people against the constitution, the Federalists wanted to construct a constitutional shield against the people's own potential myopia, injustice, irresponsibility, irrationality, and stupidity. While the former viewed the people as superior to the constitution, the latter thought, conversely, that the constitution is of a higher order than the people. "If men were angels ," Madison wrote,

> no government would be necessary. If angels were to govern men, neither external nor internal controls of government would be necessary. In fram-

ing a government which is to be administered by men over men, the great difficulty lies in this: you must first enable the government to control the governed [*sic!*]; and in the next place oblige it to control itself. A dependence on the people is, no doubt, the primary control on the government; but experience has taught mankind the necessity of auxiliary precautions.[14]

Among these "auxiliary precautions" the constitution plays a pivotal role. Its primary commission is, of course, to enable the people to govern itself, that is, to establish procedures and rules according to which the multitude of isolated individuals can transform themselves into a political body. But what is perhaps even more portentous is its function to spare individuals from the heavy burden of being downright virtuous citizens. While a polity which is grounded on the self-rule of the citizenry must expect individuals to act on all occasions according to the demanding and high-minded commands of civic morality, a polity which relies on the operation of a constitution can accept selfishness, greed, dishonesty, myopia, and all the other morally dubious qualities of individuals if only it finds the appropriate institutional design to convert private vices into public benefits — just as Bernard de Mandeville articulated,[15] and as Immanuel Kant echoed when he postulated that the perfect republic is the one in which even devils can coexist.[16] Consequently, the U.S. Constitution begins with "We the people, in order to form a more perfect union, . . . *do ordain and establish this Constitution*" — the American people utilized the Constitution as a means of self-enlightenment and self-perfection, which says: Without the Constitution and its self-binding character there could neither be "a more perfect union," nor would the people be able to "establish justice, insure domestic tranquility, provide for the common defense, promote the general welfare, and secure the blessings of liberty to ourselves and our posterity."

Contrary to what is frequently presumed, Rousseau is also not so naive as to believe in an innate, quasi-natural capacity of human beings to form a perfect polity. But once the principle of popular sovereignty, that is, the doctrine of self-rule, has been acknowledged and established, there is no way to ask if the law which the people give themselves can be unjust, "because no one is unjust to himself."[17] However, Rousseau was well aware of the fact that to possess supreme power unfortunately does not necessarily mean be endowed with supreme wisdom, justice, and benevolence. On the other hand, the opposite strategy, namely, to replace the sovereign will of the people with the smooth operation of a constitutional device, was hardly a way out of this difficulty. This was essentially the solution of the Federalists, in that they tried to minimize the negative influence of the people's inherent weaknesses on the polity by controlling their effects rather than by removing their causes. It meant to dismiss the possibly utopian idea that democratic self-rule could generate and release collective reason. If this idea is carried out to its extreme consequence, then indeed the people is absorbed, as it were, by the constitution and its institutions. The people would simply disappear as a vital and vibrant force in the life of the polity. This strategy would be the extreme antithesis to the contention that the political essence of the people rests in its preconstitutional state in which it is able to develop a general will.

In the days of the utmost tension of Russia's constitutional crisis in March 1993, President Yeltsin was quoted as saying, "I have made my choice. I leave my fate in the hands of the most just and supreme judge, the people."[18] This is the invocation of the people as the ultimate arbiter in a political impasse. The people's voice has replaced God's verdict, and since in a democracy there is indeed no power greater than the people, this is an entirely understandable statement insofar as it refers to the *supremacy* of the people ("supreme judge"). Still, the people's supremacy does not necessarily involve its untainted *justice*. Moreover, the contention that the people's supremacy is the best qualification for its role as a "most just judge" is by no means beyond doubt. Perhaps it is better to be endowed with powerlessness than with supreme power in order to best dispense justice.

Be that as it may, even if the manias, catastrophes, and megacrimes of the twentieth century have taught us to be extremely suspicious about the widespread optimism that the supreme power of the people involves supreme wisdom, justice, virtue, and integrity, we must recognize that in fact the people cannot be replaced by any other candidate as the ultimate source of legitimation in the realm of politics. But as the two extreme approaches mentioned so far clearly show, neither the concept of a prepolitical quasinatural people which encompasses the secularized qualities of a God nor its antithesis, the absorption of the people in a system of institutional rules, procedures, and checks, grasps the essence of the constitution in a democratic polity or, for that matter, the role of the demos in a constitutional state. In order to enable the people to perform its mission as the only source of legitimation in the polity it has to be denaturalized: That is, it must be transformed from an amorphous multitude of more or less isolated individuals into one corporate entity which is able to develop and to express a will, to make decisions, to reflect, and whose members are able to discuss with each other; in other words, this formless mass must be organized. And this is what constitutions are all about.

Constitutions are instruments of collective self-organization (which makes it clear that the idea of a constituent power which creates a new order ex nihilo is a [perhaps necessary] fiction). To organize means to make distinctions, to make choices between alternative options, that is, to exclude some options for the sake of others, to adopt one preference rather than another, to impose restrictions on the liberty of individuals, to allocate resources for this goal rather than for the other. In other words, to organize means to stir up and to inspirit the manifold divergences, cleavages, and antagonisms which dominate the individuals' interests, attitudes, values, and actions in all relevant social spheres. To organize an amorphous multitude is not only constructive in that it conveys to the multitude the capacity to deliberate and to act as one body; at the same time it is also destructive in that it undermines the image and self-image of a people as being one "natural" homogeneous and coherent collectivity, which exists prior to any kind of social, economic, or political organization, which has the "natural" capacity to will, to deliberate, and to act without any kind of self-mediation and without any institutional means of self-reflection and self-revision, and which is permanently jeopardized by the danger of "degeneration" and "self-alienation." This is why romanticsts of all kinds hate not only the word "organization," but also thing it designates, namely, the denaturalization of people who undergo the process of civilization by applying the means of organization to themselves. To put it pointedly: The constitution gives birth to the people in the sense in which this notion has been developed for the concept of democracy, that is, in the sense of the demos.

Having become the demos of a polity by way of a constitution, the notion of the people more and more loses the malleability which made it possible to project all kinds of transpersonal ideas into this receptacle and to identify them with "the people." During the last two hundred years, the people has been viewed as the embodiment of such divergent ideas as, for example, the nation, humanity itself, the miserable of the world, the ideas of freedom, of equality, or of welfare, and of the idea of historical progress: In the Marxist-Leninist concept "the people" was the emissary of historical progress, and the vagueness of both the notion of people and of historical progress facilitated the usurpation of political power by those who claimed to be the genuine representative of the people and, consequently, of historical progress. While minorities' political technique of identifying with "the people" in order to obtain political power and to legitimize it in democratic terms is generally known and frequently analyzed, it may be less evident that the usurping act of a well-organized minority group by which it identifies with the "the people" is only possible, or is at least extremely facilitated, if the multitude of individuals do not dispose of the means to transform themselves into a people, that is, to make up their minds, to deliberate, to communicate, and to develop institutions through which these processes are channeled and through which they can act collectively. Both the idea of the people and the real people can easily be misused by antidemocratic minorities if the real people are, so to speak, disarmed, that is, if they are denied the instruments to watch themselves and to act upon themselves. The lack of these instruments is tantamount to the lack of a constitution.

Thus, not only is there no conceptual incompatibility between constitutionalism and democracy, but, on the contrary, there is a relation of mutual support.[19] Admittedly, there is still the fact that the constitution frequently operates counter to the democratic principle of majority rule (for instance, when the constitution allows a court to overrule the majority's will as it is expressed in a law).[20] Although there is certainly a tension between constitutionalism and democracy, the more serious problem is the lack of a constitution altogether or the existence of a constitution which, for lack of self-adjustment to new historical circumstances, ceases to be an appropriate problem-solving institutional device. With respect to the constitutional problems of the most advanced industrial countries, such as Germany, this problem is addressed in the last chapter of this book. But in order to fully understand the significance of constitutionalism and of constitutions, it is equally important to analyze their role in the advent of a completely new political world in Western, central, and Eastern Europe. Is it not an enormous advance in the history of Europe that, with the tragic exception of former Yugoslavia, both political and nonpolitical conflicts within the European states are now processed within the framework and with the active use of manifold institutional instruments of constitutions. Indeed, this has been essentially accomplished by standards of legally binding rules which impose their rationality on all actors, regardless of their actual power, including the rationality that these rules can be changed, but only according to these very rules.

It has rightly been observed many times that the power struggle between the Russian president and the Russian Congress of Deputies which has been waged since the breakdown of the Soviet Union is a struggle between the exponents of a policy of radical marketization and the antiliberal forces of extremely divergent origin, namely, the old Russian nationalists and the economic and political cadres of the communist regime. What is easily overlooked is the fact that this struggle is being carried out in the context and in the terms of a constitutional struggle. The distribution of power between the president, the government, the Congress of Deputies, and the Constitutional Court, or the right of the political elite to appeal to the people for an authoritative decision, that is, the right to conduct a referendum or other forms of plebiscitary will-formation—all these questions are of course constitutional issues. It is not likely that the actors in this struggle entered into a contract in which they promised each other to act only within the constitution and to shape their respective objectives only in terms of fundamental constitutional requirements (such as to abstain from the use or threat of physical force, to acknowledge the authority of the courts).

It is the essence of political battles that the tensions and disagreement become so intense, hostile, and irreconcilable that contracts of this kind, even if made beforehand, are rarely kept. Much less can we expect them to be concluded after the political fight has begun. If, despite the circumstances which normally lead the actors of an intense political dispute to dismiss legal rules, the main issues of the fight are defined in constitutional terms, then this is a strong indication that in the minds of the relevant actors the concept of constitutionalism has attained the quality of an idea which is able to contribute to the understanding of the present situation and to the solution of the problems which it entails. Of course I do not mean to say that the looming potentiality of a civil war can always under any circumstances be thwarted if only the conflict can be translated into the language of constitutionalism. But, indeed, the very idea of constitutionalism is that it offers the participants of even the most intense political conflict an alternative to civil war other than the Hobbesian Leviathan. It is the alternative of deliberately using the people's creative capacities to solve the problems which arise whenever a multitude of potentially very divergent people happen to live together within the boundaries of a common territory and therefore have no choice but to form a polity. There is reason to believe that ever more people realize that in fact the contemporary situation does not limit our options to the Hobbesian alternative between civil war and the omnipotence of the Leviathan.

Whereas the Leviathan was conceived by Thomas Hobbes as the solution to the agonizing problem of civil war, it very soon turned out that this solution itself became the origin of new problems. Some of these problems are normally solved by the concept of constitutionalism, for instance, the problem of centralized and unlimited power. But there are many others for which a constitution itself is not a solution, for instance, economic misery and cultural deprivation for broad segments of society, the immense production of harmful side effects of economic growth, or ecological devastation. Not surprisingly, there have been suggestions to erect a dictatorship in order to solve these problems in a manner similar to the way the Leviathan mastered the civil war, namely, by the unrestrained accumulation and centralization of power (including the vast application of physical force). Just as the communist regimes were devised as the solutions to the "social question," the idea of an "ecodictatorship" has been proposed by some people as the solution to the "ecological question." Constitutionalism is not competing with these kinds of "solutions," which turned out to be false solutions or probably even themselves the problems. What makes constitutionalism an attractive alternative is not the claim to be the solution to the diverse problems of a polity at the end of the twentieth century but the well-founded assumption that it is able to liberate the problem-solving capacities which are slumbering in society.

To be sure, this is a defense of constitutionalism which is more skeptical than it appears at first glance. It presupposes that only the understanding of our limited political capacities will be able to make a creative use of the potential of constitutionalism. This is a far cry from the dawn of modern constitutionalism, when the certain knowledge of an unlimited progress of reason, of human development, of economic growth, and of technical perfection was the stimulus for the struggle for constitutions. In these early days constitutions were the weapon of reason against the darkness and stupidity of political absolutism. At the end of the twentieth century this rationale of constitutionalism no longer holds—and yet, its importance as a concept for the rational organization of a polity has by no means decreased. At least it is possible to speak of a renaissance of the idea of constitutionalism at the end of the twentieth century. In the following chapters I try to give an admittedly selective account of the developmental stages from the early enthusiastic idea to the contemporary skeptical understanding, which entails the concept of a reflexive constitutionalism of the kind which I sketch in the last chapter.

Notes

1. For a brief account of this pattern see U. K. Preuss, "Constitutional Powermaking for the New Polity: Some Deliberations on the Relations between Constituent Power and the Constitution," *Cardozo Law Review* 14, no. 639 (1993).
2. See Preuss, "Constitutional Powermaking for the New Polity."
3. For a general account of the interrelations of facticity and validity in modern constitutional reasoning see J. Habermas, *Facticity and Validity* (Frankfurt am Main, 1993).
4. H. J. Berman, *Law and Revolution: The Formation of the Western Legal Tradition* (Cambridge and London, 1983), 205ff, 395ff.
5. See H. Arendt, "Civil Disobedience," in *Crises of the Republic* (New York and London, 1969), 85ff.

6. E.-J. Sieyès, *What Is the Third Estate?* (1789; reprint, New York, 1963), 58.
7. J.-J. Rousseau, *The Social Contract*, trans. and introduced by M. Cranston (1762; reprint, London and New York, 1968), bk. 2, ch. 7, 84.
8. B. Ackerman, "Constitutional Politics/Constitutional Law," *Yale Law Journal* 99 (1989): 453–547.
9. For the consequences of this distinction for the problem of privatization of property in the postcommunist countries see U. K. Preuss, "Die Rolle des Rechtsstaates in der Transformation postkommunistischer Gesellschaften," *Rechtstheorie* 24, nos. 1–2 (1993): 181–204.
10. This question is addressed by S. Holmes, "Back to the Drawing Board," *East European Constitutional Review* 2, no. 1 (Winter 1993): 21–25, 21.
11. For the American case see J. Nedelsky, *Private Property and the Limits of American Constitutionalism: The Madisonian Framework and Its Legacy* (Chicago and London, 1990), 68–75.
12. See C. Schmitt, *The Concept of the Political* (New Brunswick, N. J., 1976).
13. Rousseau, *The Social Contract*, bk. 2, ch. 1, 70.
14. A. Hamilton, J. Madison, J. Jay, *The Federalist Papers*, introduction by C. Rossiter (New York, 1961), no. 51, 322.
15. See B. d. Mandeville's 1714 treatise *The Fable of the Bees* (New York, 1962); the underlying paradigm is analyzed by A. O. Hirschman, *The Passions and the Interests* (Princeton, 1977), 18–19.
16. I. Kant, *Zum ewigen Frieden: Zweiter Abschnitt. Erster Zusatz. Werkausgabe*, ed., W. Weischedel, Vol. 11 (Frankfurt am Main, 1977), 224.
17. Rousseau, *The Social Contract*, bk. 2, ch. 6, 82.
18. *International Herald Tribune*, Frankfurt ed., 27–28 March, p. 1.
19. See, e.g., S. Holmes, "Precommitment and the Paradox of Democracy," in J. Elster and R. Slagstad, eds., *Constitutionalism and Democracy* (Cambridge, 1988), 195–240.
20. See, e.g., the discussion of this problem by L. H. Tribe, *Constitutional Law*, 2nd ed. (Mineola, 1988), 10.

✧1✧

The Constitution as the "Object of All Longing"

"Our great and sacred Constitution, serene and inviolable, stretches its beneficent powers over our land... like the outstretched arm of God himself.... O Marvelous Constitution... Maker, Monitor, Guardian of Mankind."[1] This "Te Deum" to the U.S. Constitution (as a commentator tartly described it) was offered by a New York attorney named Henry R. Estabrook in 1913. Presumably his words struck some as a shade eccentric even at the time; all the same, they can be considered representative of the thinking—or perhaps it would be more accurate to say the feelings—on the Constitution of countless jurists and politicians of the era. These lofty sentiments, intoned with such solemnity as to verge on the ridiculous, reflect the atmosphere of holy zeal prevailing after the Civil War in particular, when Americans' belief that their nation had been granted elect status by divine authority became combined with the patriotic legends of its constitutional origins;[2] this belief accompanied America's entry onto the stage of world politics and, indeed, may have made that entry possible. If we compare this quasi-religious fervor with the levelheaded pragmatism so correctly stressed as typical of the Founding Fathers at the end of the eighteenth century, then there is a strong temptation to dismiss it as an expression of national chauvinism that merits no special attention, since it can be found everywhere. The temptation is all the greater when we consider that the quotation dates from the "Lochner Era," named after a decision handed down by the U.S. Supreme Court in 1905. The decision referred to a New York law limiting bakers to a sixty-hour workweek; the high court declared it unconstitutional on the grounds that it infringed on the rights to own property and make contracts. For the next three decades this decision would serve as a model for a theory of constitutional law whose Social Darwinist tendencies were too obvious

25

to be overlooked.³ Was there not a great contradiction here? Or was the Constitution sacred because it embodied a divine plan that just happened to be identical with the interests of property owners? Such a religiously colored enthusiasm for constitutional government existed before this only during the French Revolution, in which no secret was made of the fact that it was a revolution of the property-owning middle class, at least in its first phase. Despite the high esteem in which property was held, however, the French Revolution left no doubt of the profane character of property in comparison with a constitution; that the population was ready to sacrifice its property for the higher cause of a constitution was occasionally considered not only possible but something that had actually occurred:

> From the shores of the Atlantic to the Jura, from Lille to the Pyrenees, there is a single common will. A constitution is the object of all longing. To achieve this, every citizen is sacrificing his fortune, his personal affairs, and his peace and quiet; every province, every community is shedding its privileges or its entitlements with such haste that there can be no doubt: the principles of society have been known and absorbed here for a long time.⁴

But what is it about the idea of a constitution that can call forth "a mystical sense of mission"⁵ even outside the narrow circle of "the intellectual elite involved in creating one"?⁶ Obviously in this case the revolutionary agitation is directed at a goal that could unite (at least for one brief and historic moment) the objects "of all longing" and thus "encompass within itself all forms of the good."⁷ "The good" is conceived of not as something static and complete but, rather, first and foremost as the capacity to perfect society, to improve and further develop learning, society, and morals, and to increase the use of reason; in other words, it is progress personified.⁸ In this striving a constitution represents more than just an instrument for perfecting the body politic; it becomes itself the object of an incessant striving for improvement. As a journalist wrote more than a decade before the Revolution: "Government rule approaches perfection to the degree that, by the force of its constitution, it induces even the least virtuous of its subjects to act voluntarily as the common good requires."⁹ The ideas of revolution, progress, and a constitution united to form a harmonious chord that still reverberated in the German revolution of March 1848 and carried a term previously unknown to the heights of popularity, the word *Errungenschaft* [gain, achievement]. A skeptical observer wrote in 1847 that "in the very recent past... the word *Errungenschaft* has taken on an expanded meaning in several respects," namely, "something seized with impetuous haste, not infrequently by means of public uproar and brute force."[10] The object that is to be attained with "impetuous haste" and "brute force" turns out to be nothing other than a constitution, and so it is not surprising that the same issue is presented in entirely different terms by the Constitutional Club of Berlin: "Only if the representatives of the people oppose the forces of reaction with all their might and refuse to disband until a constitution such as the people demand has actually been adopted, only then will we be able to regard the gains of our glorious March revolution and the defeat of anarchy as secure."

What is the cause of this fervent tone, and above all, how does one explain that the call for a constitution has become almost synonymous here with a striving for progress and has acquired such a close connection with a revolutionary movement? In England and on the continent of Europe the term "constitution" has a long prerevolutionary tradition, although it was originally used in the plural as "constitutions" or "fundamental constitutions."[11] From the early seventeenth century on these terms refer to the form of government and designate the fundamental laws of political rule; the plural usage originated in the Middle Ages, when society consisted of different estates with differing relationships to authority. The term "constitution" had previously referred to the physical character of a body, to its basic health or vitality; it was first applied to political and legal conditions in the seventeenth century, when the Scientific Revolution made parallels between natural and social phenomena popular. The seventeenth-century founders of modern science applied the theological and legal concept of law — with its implications of inviolable order and absolute dictates — to the regularities they observed in nature, calling them "natural laws,"[12] and conversely, terms from nature were applied to society, as in the phrase "the body politic." The condition of a body politic is its constitution: "What holds it together, what it is composed of, its head and members, what gives it unity."[13] Under the influence of theological discussions about the proper form of a church constitution, meaning the terms of association of a congregation of believers, some authors' conception of the term "constitution" acquired a certain republican flavor; in this view, a perfect constitution would consist not so much in a balance of power between ruler and ruled as in a form of unity encompassing both equally, the joining of many separate entities into one whole.[14]

Nevertheless, the plural usage of "constitutions" or "fundamental constitutions" continued in England in the seventeenth century, because after 1688 the idea prevailed there that the best guarantee of a just political order was the supremacy of Parliament over the monarch and not a law antecedent to and constituting both. As a result, the English revolutions of the seventeenth century contributed little to the emergence of the modern constitutional state in the last third of the eighteenth century. Both the American and French revolutionary movements developed their definition of the term "constitution" in sharp distinction to the English model. If American revolutionaries had any ties to English constitutional thought, it would be the resemblance of some of their ideas to those of the Levellers, that minority within Cromwell's army who produced the first written draft of a constitution in the Agreement of the People in 1647, although it was still couched in the terms of a contract.[15] To ensure that this "law paramount" would be binding even on Parliament, they demanded that it be voted on by the people, for "that which is done by one Parliament ... may be undone by the next Parliament."[16] The Levellers' views did not prevail in England, however. While the monarch was forced to abdicate in 1688 as a result of accusations that he had violated the "constitution of the kingdom,"[17] this reasoning implied that James had violated the rights of Parliament, not that a law existed to which Parliament was also subordinate.[18] (When the term "Parliament" is used in English constitutional law, it refers to its three constitutive elements: the Crown, the House of Lords, and the House of Commons.)[19] The Glorious Revolution marks the beginning of the era in which parliamentary sovereignty supplanted for good the idea of a "paramount law."[20] No limitations were imposed on Parliament's power to legislate; the laws it passed had the same status as the rules according to which they were passed, since Parliament had the right to establish both. William Blackstone, the most influential English legal commentator of the eighteenth century, wrote:

> It [Parliament] can regulate or new model the succession to the crown; ... it can change and create afresh even the constitution of the kingdom and of parliament themselves.... It can, in short, do everything that is not naturally impossible; and therefore some have not scrupled to call its power, by a figure rather too bold, the omnipotence of parliament.[21]

Since "ordinary" and "fundamental" laws had no distinction in ranking or precedence, the latter concept had no legal significance. An

American author writing in 1775 found it outrageous and incomprehensible that the English Bill of Rights and Acts of Settlement had no higher status than a law "which established a turnpike road." It was the implication of this — that the liberties of the people depended "upon nothing more permanent or established than the vague, rapacious, or interested inclination of a majority of five hundred and fifty-eight men"[22] — which led the American settlers to declare their independence and develop their own notion of a constitution, one which remains in force to the present day.

The objection that parliamentary sovereignty guaranteed neither individual rights nor a just political order touched on a sore spot in every concept of sovereignty. A person or group can be granted supreme and unchecked power of legislation over all the rest of the people only if law is something inherently reasonable, to which everyone will submit by virtue of his own innate reason. If every expression of the legislator's will becomes law solely because he has the power to enforce it, then the concept of law ceases to have any relation to justice; the sovereign's will is binding even if it is unreasonable and unjust. This was Hobbes's famous reply to the internal contradiction posed by law established by a supremely sovereign legislator:

> That Law can never be against Reason, our Lawyers are agreed; . . .
> And it is true: but the doubt is, of whose Reason it is, that shall be
> received for Law. It is not meant of any private Reason; for then
> there would be as much contradiction in the Lawes, as there is in
> the Schooles; . . . therefore it is not that *Juris prudentia*, or wisdome
> of subordinate Judges; but the Reason of this our Artificiall Man
> the Commonwealth, and his Command, that maketh Law.[23]

The Latin version of 1670 of *Leviathan* puts it even more succinctly: "Doctrinae quidem verae esse possunt; sed authoritas, non veritas, facit legem.[24] It was the American colonists' practical experience of this doctrine that prompted them to search for counterarguments. They responded that certain fundamental principles and laws ought to be declared to be above and beyond the reach of Parliament's will, on the basis of their inherent reasonableness and evident truth. This is the basic distinction between laws and a constitution. All expressions of the legislator's will were laws, but a constitution — and here the concept is quite clearly understood in the singular form — contains the principles that limit and bind this will. It is both more than and different from a "form of government." "All countries have some form of government," proclaimed an anonymous American writer in 1776, "but few, or perhaps none, have truly a Constitution."[25] In this view, the mother country England also lacked a constitution. "In England," wrote Thomas Paine in 1791, "it is not difficult to perceive that everything has a constitution, except the nation," since there, supreme authority was vested in Parliament rather than in a constitution voted on by the nation and binding on any elected government. "A constitution is the property of a nation, and not of those who exercise the government."[26]

A constitution was characterized by three crucial elements. First and foremost, a constitution must list the fundamental principles and individual rights which lawmakers were bound to respect because they were, in the words of the American Declaration of Independence of 1776, "truths" held to be "self-evident." A constitution represented a fundamental document because it was a codification of truth.[27] From this two principles with practical legal consequences could be derived. First, the lawmakers' powers had limits imposed from without, and second, these powers derived solely from the constitution, since the lawmaking assembly itself came into existence only through the constitution. With this step the understanding of a constitution that had prevailed up to that time — namely that it was a contract between the government and the governed — was superseded. Paine expressed a truth empirically evident to Americans: that constitutions are contracts of the people with one another through which a government is first called into being. "To suppose that any government can be a party in a compact with the whole people, is to suppose it to have existence before it can have a right to exist," he wrote[28] — a rather laconic statement of the truly revolutionary idea that political sovereignty is first created by a constitution and is not a preexisting entity whose powers a constitution merely limits.[29] This conviction was so deeply entrenched in the minds of the majority of the delegates to the Constitutional Convention meeting in Philadelphia that in the summer of 1787 they rejected a proposal to include a Bill of Rights in the Constitution. They argued that since the Constitution permitted no infringement of citizens' rights, and since the public authorities had only those powers that had been specifically delegated to them, making a catalogue of such rights would be superfluous and perhaps even directly harmful. If through an oversight the catalogue happened to be incomplete, lawmakers might conclude that they could legitimately curtail those rights that had been omitted.[30] The second crucial element of the evolving modern definition of a constitution was its normative character. While this is taken for granted today, its development over the seventeenth and eighteenth centuries was gradual. As mentioned above, the term "constitution" originally signified no more than the actual condition of a body politic, and even when it came to be understood to mean an "instrument of government," it tended to be used descriptively, to characterize an existing system of government, rather than prescriptively. Of course, political philosophers — above all Rousseau in France — had created a system of legitimate political authority derived from natural law, but until the first attempts were made to frame a constitution during the French Revolution it remained a purely theoretical construct.[31] The Americans, by contrast, had become clearly aware of the normative character of a constitution in their struggle against English parliamentary absolutism. After years of battling Parliament, they were interested not only in what "eternal" and "sacred" philosophical principles might bind lawmakers but also in the binding force of a higher law, whose infringement would give a people the right to rebel. However, even more important than this idea, which was already familiar to students of philosophy and natural law, was the dynamic of social change set in motion by applying the principle of normativity. A constitution's normative quality not only functions as a more or less passive yardstick for assessing social reality, it also creates a demand "that its provisions be put into practice. In other words, it looks to the future."[32] One consequence of this is that every state of affairs not conforming to the norms established by the constitution loses its legitimacy. But even more important, the codifying of ethical principles in the form of constitutional norms becomes a call to alter reality to correspond to them, to make society as coherent and rational as the document.[33] A constitution thus becomes a legally binding blueprint for constructing a rational society;[34] rather than reflecting social conditions, it proposes to model them on its own image.[35] With the notion of a constitution, philosophy had acquired, in a manner of speaking, an instrument with which it could not only interpret the world but also alter it.

The normative aspect of a constitution is intimately connected with its codification in a single written document. Its foundation on eternal truths made it fundamentally superior to a hodgepodge of individual laws and virtually demanded expression as a coherent and systematic entity; this form alone would help to make it the standard for judging the whole spectrum of social phenomena. It was essential to avoid ambiguity in formulating these principles, and this could best be achieved by fixing it in writing in a single document. Even in Germany, where the existence of dozens of principalities had created a mosaic of different social and legal conditions, Johann Christian Majer observed in his *Teutsches weltliches Staatsrecht* [Civil Law of German States] of 1775 that "as culture progresses in general . . . naturally the prestige of formal written constitutions, their number, precision, necessity, and usefulness have increased in equal measure."[36] How much more must this apply to America, where a commercial middle class had created more unified conditions, and also to France and the systematic rationalism of French political theory. Furthermore, the notion that a constitution can be written down clearly reveals a link to Protestant belief in the authority of Scripture or Holy Writ. Referring to the constitution of the state of Pennsylvania, Paine gives a very vivid description of how these ideas are connected:

> It was the political bible of the state. Scarcely a family was without it. Every member of the government had a copy; and nothing was more common, when any debate arose on the principle of a bill, or on the extent of any species of authority, than for the members to take the printed constitution out of their pocket, and read the chapter with which such matter in debate was connected.[37]

This passage suggests that the constitution had the same status for American settlers and their political intentions that Luther's translation of the Bible had for German Protestants. If political sovereignty was to be vested in the people, then the act through which the people established political powers and granted them lasting authority had to be something that everyone could see with his own eyes. The French National Assembly expressed this thought emphatically in the Preamble to its Declaration of the Rights of Man and of the Citizen of 1789:

> The representatives of the French people, organized in the National Assembly, considering that *ignorance, forgetfulness* or contempt of the rights of man are the sole causes of the public miseries and of the corruption of governments, have resolved to set forth in a solemn declaration the natural, inalienable, and sacred rights of man, in order that his declaration, being *ever present* to all the members of the social body, may unceasingly *remind* them of their rights and their duties; in order that the acts of the legislative power and those of the executive power may be each moment *compared* with the aim of every political institution and thereby may be more respected; and in order that the demands of the citizens, grounded henceforth

upon *simple and incontestable principles*, may always take the direction of maintaining the constitution and the welfare of all.[38]

The existence of a constitution as a single written document is thus not merely a matter of form but an essential component of an entirely new understanding of political order. This order is founded upon universal truths, because it is derived from principles that apply to all people, and these can be solemnly stated in a written document similar to a political catechism. A constitution is thus reminiscent of ancient tablets of sacred law in both form and content,[39] and was understood in such terms in France during the revolutionary period: "A constitution must be the catechism of the human race"; "the sacred constitution" is nothing less than "the gospel of the times."[40]

Various reasons can be given for why constitutions came to be viewed as sacred. Schmale sees it in connection with the process of de-Christianization he considers characteristic of eighteenth-century France: "the 'banishment of God' from the ordinary person's daily life." Constitutions became secularized surrogates for religious doctrines of salvation, a "basis for all political and social life, and perhaps even the lives of individuals."[41] Grimm, on the other hand, uses a comparative approach and asks what objective historical conditions were necessary for societies to "constitute themselves" on the basis of a written document. He concludes that they consisted of the replacement of a fragmented feudal order by a unified state, the understanding of law as mutable according to human plans and desires, and the growth of a class of people engaged in commerce on more than a subsistence level and over large geographical areas who began to see themselves as a social unit. Their ideas of justice came to be based on the principle of equal individual freedom and the consequent right to act independently and conduct transactions on a voluntary basis. In other words, constitutions in the modern sense — that is, comprehensive, normative, and written rules establishing and limiting government authority and guaranteeing individual rights — could be produced only by the modern bourgeoisie.[42]

While I do not wish to challenge these explanations, I do consider it necessary to place more emphasis on the connection between the idea of a constitution and the notion of progress. It is hardly surprising that both the American colonists and the French representatives of the Third Estate considered their revolutions to represent progress. (I would like to postpone discussion of the different terms in which they understood "progress" for the moment.) It is less immediately obvious, however, why a constitution appeared to them as the best way to secure their revolutionary gains. During the revolutions "the people" appeared as direct participants on the political stage, giving tangible expression to the principle of democracy. A constitution, on the other hand, acts as an intermediary between the people and the exercise of power; all political authority derives from it, and as a fundamental law it expressly limits the power of the popularly elected assembly. It thus appears as if constitutions work against the very conditions that led to their adoption. In particular, it has remained unclear to the present day how the right of the people freely to determine their own destiny, which was claimed in the revolutions of the eighteenth century, is compatible with the limitations on these rights imposed by the constitutions these same revolutions produced. How do we reconcile the fact that the founding fathers proclaimed the principle of popular sovereignty while simultaneously binding succeeding generations to their own will as laid down in the constitution?

Paradoxically, the modern concept of a constitution, while inseparably linked to the principle of popular sovereignty, is also characterized by the expectation of lasting, perhaps even eternal, duration. Even in the predemocratic epoch the notion of a fundamental law as something antecedent to other laws contained a striving for permanence. "Constitutions" based on contracts between princes and estates possessed such permanence insofar as they could be altered only with the agreement of both parties; that is, the ruler could not abolish them unilaterally. As we have seen, however, Paine argued that modern constitutions are not understood as contractual agreements between different parties to power but, rather, as an act of the people, the origin of all political authority. Both Hobbes and Rousseau had agreed that no sovereign could be bound by promises or laws he had imposed on himself.[43]

If democratic constitutions nonetheless "rival the *lex aeterna* of the Stoic-Christian legal hierarchy in their claims to permanence,"[44] this is above all because they claim to represent eternal and therefore equally sacred truths. The last article of the Fundamental Constitutions of Carolina of 1669 as revised by John Locke (retaining the old plural usage) proclaims: "These Fundamental Constitutions shall be and remain the sacred and *unalterable* form and rule of government of Carolina *forever*."[45] The Preamble to the Virginia Bill of Rights of 12 June 1776 states that it is a "declaration of rights made by the representatives of the good people of Virginia, . . . which rights do pertain to them and their posterity, as the basis and form of government." The first section then goes on to state that "all men are by nature equally free and independent and have certain inherent rights, of which ... they cannot, by any compact, deprive or divest their posterity." Immediately following this, however, Section 2 declares that "all power is vested in, and consequently derived from, the people."[46] The Preamble to the Constitution of the United States also states the framers' intention to "secure the Blessings of Liberty to ourselves and our posterity" without conceding one iota of the principle of popular sovereignty.

Several years after his work on the constitution of Carolina, however, Locke wrote in his *Second Treatise of Government* that, while everyone is under the obligation of engagements or promises he has made for himself, he "*cannot* by any *Compact* whatsoever bind *his Children* or posterity. For this Son, when a Man, being altogether as free as the Father, *any act of the Father can no more give away the liberty of the Son*, than it can of any body else."[47] Here a contradiction seems to exist between the proclamation of the eternal and unalterable validity of the constitution of Carolina and a violation of natural law represented by any binding of a future generation to particular terms. If a constitution is indeed unalterable and remains in force forever, then later generations do not have the freedom to amend it according to their own notions of freedom and happiness; they are bound by the decisions of their long-deceased forefathers.[48] This contradiction was not lost on either the founders of constitutional democracies or later observers, and for this reason a number of them spoke out directly against claiming eternal validity for such documents. The most famous of these statements is no doubt Article 28 of the French Constitution of the Year I, the Declaration of the Rights of Man and of the Citizen drawn up by the National Convention in 1793: "A people has always the right to review, to reform, and to alter its constitution. One generation cannot subject to its law the future generations."[49]

If one considers the grounds on which the binding of future generations by the framers of a constitution was opposed, it is striking how consistently they were connected with the idea of progress. Thomas Jefferson wrote a letter containing the following passage in the year 1816, that is, fully aware of the events of the French Revolution:

Laws and institutions must go hand in hand with the progress of the human mind. As that becomes more developed, more enlightened, as new discoveries are made, new truths disclosed, and manners and opinions change with the change of circumstances, institutions must advance also, and keep pace with the times.[50]

Kant had argued in similar terms more than thirty years earlier:

> The people of one epoch cannot form an alliance and conspire to prevent people of a later epoch from increasing their knowledge, correcting their errors, and becoming more enlightened in general. This would be a crime against human nature, which had been ordained from the beginning to progress in just such a way. Later generations are thus perfectly justified in regarding such resolutions as unauthorized and irresponsibly enacted, and in overturning them. . . . A person can delay acquiring enlightenment on matters he is required to know, but only for a limited period of time; to deprive himself of enlightenment permanently is to violate and trample on the sacred rights of man, and this is all the more the case if he deprives posterity.[51]

Kant's argument against declaring a constitution eternally valid and unalterable is here not — as the French would later proclaim — that it violates the freedom of every following generation to decide for itself. Instead, Kant's argument is similar to those of Jefferson, Paine, and others that any binding of future generations to a constitution approved by their forefathers must be rejected because it is to be feared that this would prevent humanity from acquiring further knowledge and exclude the possibility of social progress.[52] If human nature "has been ordained from the beginning" to increase its degree of enlightenment, then according to the internal logic of this argument a constitution declared unalterable by its framers but preserving all the conditions for such improvement and progress to be possible would not violate the rights of future generations. Evidently this must have been the reasoning of those framers who, without showing the slightest awareness of a contradiction, simultaneously proclaimed the principle of popular sovereignty *and* the binding nature of a constitution on future generations. According to their logic, a constitution represented not an impediment to progress but, rather, an eternal medium for progress to be continual. In fact it was not possible to envision a higher truth than that expressed in the American Declaration of Independence that "all men are created equal; that they are endowed by their Creator with certain inalienable rights; that among these are life, liberty, and the pursuit of happiness"; what kind of progress could be supposed to occur in this regard? It should be noted that neither are the inalienable rights themselves considered to be the result of progress; men were endowed with them "by their Creator," that is, they are eternal and unaffected by historical change, whereas progress is a historical category. What makes these rights sacred is the circumstance that recognizing them *creates the conditions under which progress becomes possible*. Establishing the rights to life, liberty, and the pursuit of happiness represents genuine progress beyond oppression through unjust rule, but once they have been established, they cannot undergo further perfection; rather than describing a particular state or condition, they open up a world of varied and undefined possibilities. Only when these rights are respected are people in a position to "increase their knowledge, correct their errors, and become more enlightened in general." And since this state has been ordained for mankind, its continuation must be guaranteed forever. This is what a constitution accomplishes; it is both historically unique and sacred because it creates a lasting possibility for human progress, and for this reason it can and must take the form of a written law. In its form as a fundamental law it guarantees the consistency, predictability, and permanence of an eternal and invariable order, whereas its content unleashes the dynamics of permanent change, indeed the transformation of a society and the many possible forms it may choose to take. In short, a constitution permits a society to benefit from change and to enjoy security at the same time, to experience progress as continuity.

It is possible to interpret the American Revolution and the aims of the U.S. Constitution in such terms. In France, however, the relationship between progress and a constitution was understood differently, just as the French and American revolutions took fundamentally different courses.

Notes

1. Cited according to A. M. Bickel, *The Supreme Court and the Idea of Progress* (New Haven and London, 1978), 15.
2. See C. Frankenberg and U. Rödel, *Von der Volkssouveränität zum Minderheitenschutz: Die Freiheit der Kommunikation im Verfassungsstaat* (Frankfurt, 1981), 246ff; M. Mathiopoulos, *Amerika: Das Experiment des Fortschritts. Ein Vergleich des politischen Denkens in den USA und Europa* (Paderborn, 1987), 87ff.
3. See Tribe, *American Constitutional Law*, 570.
4. From the journal *Révolutions de Paris*, no. 20 (21–28 November 1789); cited according to W. Schmale, *Entchristianisierung, Revolution, und*

Verfassung: Zur Mentalitätsgeschichte der Verfassung in Frankreich, 1715–1794 (Berlin, 1988).

5. K. Loewenstein, "Verfassung," in C. D. Kernig, ed., Marxismus im Systemvergleich (Frankfurt and New York, 1973), col. 274.
6. Schmale, Entchristianisierung, Revolution, und Verfassung, 57ff.
7. From a contemporary source, cited according to Schmale, ibid., 59.
8. See R. Koselleck, "Fortschrift," in O. Brunner et al., eds., Geschichtliche Grundbegriffe 2 (Stuttgart, 1975), 351ff, 372ff.
9. Cited according to Schmale, Entchristianisierung, Revolution, und Verfassung, 52.
10. This and the following citation are taken from E. Matthias and H. Schierbaum, Errungenschaften: Zur Geschichte eines Schlagwortes unserer Zeit (Ilm and Munich, 1961), 4.
11. For more on the subject see C. Stourzh, "Staatsformenlehre und Fundamentalgesetze in England und Nordamerika im 17. und 18. Jahrhundert: Zur Genese des modernen Verfassungsbegriffs," in R. Verhaus, ed., Herrschaftsverträge, Wahlkapitulationen, Fundamentalgesetze (Göttingen, 1977), 294ff.
12. See E. Zilsel, Die sozialen Ursprünge der neuzeitlichen Wissenschaft, 2nd ed., ed. W. Krohn (Frankfurt, 1985), 66ff. See also the editor's introduction, p. 8.
13. Stourzh, "Staatsformenlehre," 307.
14. Ibid., 306–7.
15. For more on the constitutional ideas of the Levellers see J. W. Gough, Fundamental Law in English Constitutional History (Oxford, 1955), 112ff. See also H.-C. Schröder, "Die amerikanische und die englische Revolution in vergleichender Perspektive," in H.-U Wehler, ed., Zweihundert Jahre amerikanische Revolution und moderne Revolutionsforschung (Göttingen, 1976), 35, and C. Hill, Some Intellectual Consequences of the English Revolution (London, 1980).
16. Cited according to J. R. MacCormack, Revolutionary Politics in the Long Parliament (Cambridge, Mass., 1973), 313.
17. See D. Grimm, "Verfassung (II)," in O. Brunner, et al., eds., Geschichtliche Grundbegriffe 6 (Stuttgart, 1990), 865–66.
18. Compare the text of the accusations against the king in Gough, Fundamental Law, 78.
19. W. Blackstone, Commentaries on the Laws of England (facsimile edition of the edition of 1765; Chicago and London, 1979), 1, 155.
20. Gough, Fundamental Law, 160ff; see also R. Wahl, "Der Vorrang der Verfassung," Der Staat (1981): 485ff, 488ff.
21. Blackstone, Commentaries, 1, 156.
22. Cited according to G. S. Wood, The Creation of the American Republic 1776–1787 (New York, 1972), 266.
23. T. Hobbes, Leviathan (Harmondsworth, 1968), pt. 2, ch. 26, sec. 7, 316–17.
24. T. Hobbes, Leviathan: Sive de Materia, Forma, et Potestate Civitatis ecclesiasticae et Civilis III (London, 1841), Caput 26, 202.
25. Cited according to Wood, The Creation of the American Republic, 267.

26. T. Paine, *Rights of Man* (Harmondsworth, 1984), pt. 2, ch. 4, 191.
27. See H. Hofmann, "Zur Idee des Staatsgrundgesetzes," in H. Hofmann, ed., *Recht Politik — Verfassung: Studien zur Geschichte der politischen Philosophie* (Frankfurt, 1986), 285.
28. Paine, *Rights of Man*, pt. 2, ch. 4, 188.
29. D. Grimm, "Entstehungs- und Wirkungsbedingungen des modernen Konstitutionalismus," in D. Simon, ed., *Akten des 26. Deutschen Rechtshistorikertages* (Frankfurt, 1987), 45ff.
30. See the report on the debates in Wood, *The Creation of the American Republic*, 536ff. The American Bill of Rights was not included in the Constitution until 1791, in the form of the first ten amendments.
31. See R. Redslob, *Die Staatstheorien der französischen Nationalversammlung von 1789* (Leipzig, 1912) for details.
32. E. Schmidt-Assmann, *Der Verfassungsbegriff in der deutschen Staatslehre der Aufklärung und des Historismus* (Berlin, 1967), 58.
33. Ibid., 199.
34. Hofmann, "Zur Idee des Staatsgrundgesetzes," 290ff.
35. Grimm, "Entstehungs- und Wirkungsbedingungen des modernen Konstitutionalismus," 49.
36. Cited according to Hofmann, "Zur Idee des Staatsgrundgesetzes," 276.
37. Paine, *Rights of Man*, pt. 2, ch. 4, 187.
38. Author's emphasis. Cited according to F. M. Anderson, ed., *The Constitutions and Other Select Documents Illustrative of the History of France, 1789–1907*, 2nd ed. (New York, 1908), 15, 59.
39. Hofmann, "Zur Idee des Staatsgrundgesetzes," 261ff, 286; see also 264–65, 269, 280ff; and Grimm, "Verfassung (II)."
40. Cited according to Schmale, *Entchristianisierung, Revolution, und Verfassung*, 13.
41. Ibid., 20, 57, and passim.
42. Grimm, "Entstehungs- und Wirkungsbedingungen des modernen Konstitutionalismus," 50ff.
43. Hobbes, *Leviathan*, pt. 2, ch. 26, 313; Rousseau, *The Social Contract*, bk. 1, ch. 7, 62.
44. Hofmann, "Zur Idee des Staatsgrundgesetzes," 286.
45. Fundamental Constitutions of Carolina (1669) in F. N. Thorpe, ed., *The Federal and State Constitutions, Colonial Charters, and Other Organic Laws* (Washington, D.C., 1909), 5, 2786.
46. Virginia Bill of Rights (1776), in Thorpe, ed., *The Federal and State Constitutions*, 7, 3812–13.
47. On the dating of Locke's *Two Treatises of Government* see P. Laslett's foreword to the student edition (Cambridge, Eng., 1988), 58ff. Quotation from bk. 2, ch. 8, par. 116, 346.
48. For more on this point see the extensive and well-documented study by S. Holmes, "Precommitment and the Paradox of Democracy," in J. Elster and R. Slagstad, eds., *Constitutionalism and Democracy* (Cambridge, Eng., 1988), 195–240.
49. Anderson, ed., *Select Documents Illustrative of the History of France*, 174.

50. Cited according to Holmes, "Precommitment and the Paradox of Democracy," 205–6.
51. I. Kant, "Beantwortung der Frage: Was ist Aufklärung?," in *Werke* (Frankfurt, 1977), 11, 57–58 [my translation — DLS].
52. See Holmes, "Precommitment and the Paradox of Democracy," 205ff, 238ff.

✧ 2 ✧

Social Progress or Political Freedom?

Surprisingly, the American Revolution and the creation of the U.S. Constitution stimulated the imagination of contemporaries far less than the French Revolution did.[1] In 1798 — almost ten years after the Third Estate had proclaimed itself the National Assembly and more than a year before the 18th of Brumaire — Kant wrote:

> The revolution of a brilliant people which we have seen unfolding in our day may succeed or fail; it may be so filled with misery and atrocities that a right-thinking person who could have hopes of bringing it off successfully if he were to attempt it a second time would still never decide to do so, since the cost of the experiment would be too high. — This revolution, I say, finds in the minds of all those watching it (who are not entangled in this game themselves) a wish to participate that borders on enthusiasm, and since merely revealing this attitude could have had dangerous consequences, it must be caused by a moral disposition in the human race.[2]

With these cautious but unmistakable words Kant described the French Revolution as a "historical sign" demonstrating nothing less than a tendency in humankind to progress toward its own improvement. And he sees this moral cause in the striving for a republican constitution, "which is not to be achieved by fierce struggles alone," but which Kant firmly believes will be achieved in the future. Even if the Revolution were to fail and society returned to its former condition, his "philosophical prediction" would lose none of its validity; "such a phenomenon in human history will never be forgotten," wrote Kant, "because it has revealed a disposition and a capacity in human nature for improvement."[3]

It must be this stirring belief in the capacity of human nature to

41

better itself that has given the French Revolution its unique place in history, despite the Reign of Terror. It has come to be seen as the paradigm of a truly modern revolution, even though its independent or lasting contributions to the development of constitutional law seem few — at least at first glance. The idea of a written constitution that establishes a comprehensive political order, both guaranteeing basic rights and providing for the separation of powers, was not a discovery of the French Revolution.[4] "Any society in which the guarantee of the rights is not secured, or the separation of powers not determined, has no constitution at all." This definition of a constitutional state, proclaimed so self-confidently — indeed, almost imperiously — in Article 16 of the Declaration of the Rights of Man and of the Citizen in 1789,[5] was new neither in theory nor in practice, since both elements were already to be found in the Virginia Bill of Rights of 1776 and in the constitutions of other American states modeled after it.

There can be no doubt that the example of America influenced the deliberations of the French National Assembly in 1789 in a number of ways.[6] Yet although the revolutionaries in America and France both invoked the natural rights of men who were created free and equal as they struggled to transform the political order of their day, they understood the theoretical meaning of these rights in very different terms. For the American founding fathers, the freedom and equality of all men was a fact, a given, and a political order was legitimate only to the degree that it respected this fact and protected the rights of the individual. For the French, on the other hand, freedom and equality and the rule of reason were ideals that would not become reality until the future. The aim of the rule of reason — as Maximilien Robespierre proclaimed in his speech "On the Principles of Political Morality" of 5 February 1794 — was to substitute "all the virtues and all the miracles of the Republic for all the vices and all the absurdities of the monarchy."[7] Here we can see the tendency mentioned above to use the term "republic" to mean "a future order." In Anglo-American usage in the eighteenth century, the word "republic" was generally synonymous with "constitutional government,"[8] and it played no greater role in the French Revolution either, until the abolition of the monarchy. As late as July 1791 — that is, after the king's attempt to flee had failed — Robespierre was still saying that a republic and a monarchy were not incompatible, since all that mattered was the degree of a nation's freedom.[9] But now, in 1794, the term "republic" did not mean primarily the opposite of a monarchy. For Robespierre, in contrast to the American founding fathers,[10] "republic" had become identical with "democracy,"[11] which is governed by the principles of virtue and equality, as Montesquieu had already emphasized.[12] It is, in other words, not only an institutional but also a social ideal, whose inner necessity resulted from the fact that "the convention's establishment of a centralistic republic in a major country represented an unprecedented innovation."[13] After the passage of the Loi Le Chapelier (on 14 June 1791), which denied workers and artisans the freedom to assemble and organize, a government ethic had to try to establish that minimum of social coherence which a rule based on individual freedom cannot produce of itself. Virtue and equality were the "soul of the Republic," declared Robespierre in his 1794 speech to the convention, and from this it followed

> that the first rule of your political conduct must be to relate all your actions to maintaining equality and developing virtue.... Thus what you adopt or establish should be everything which tends to arouse love of country, to purify morals, to elevate souls and to guide the passions of the human heart toward the public interest.[14]

For centuries the doctrine of the eternally recurring cycle of the forms of the government had been taught as handed down from Aristotle and his medieval disciples. The democratic *politeia* or *res publica* formed a regular part of this cycle, occurring either at its height or as a period of decadence. Now, however, it came to be seen as the high point in a linear development of humanity toward ever greater betterment; it represented the realization, in institutional form, of a philosophical program: "We want to fulfill the wishes of nature, the destinies of humanity, to keep the promises of philosophy ... in order that we may see the dawn of universal felicity!"[15] Here we see a first sign of the tension that would become evident in Marxist theory between the principle of popular sovereignty and the idea of universal progress and human rights; this is a subject to which we shall return. The final aim of the revolution and the government established by it is not popular self-determination; rather, self-determination is a means for the people to fulfill their destiny and play their foreordained role in the great plan of history. This secularized form of "salvation" was no longer concerned with reestablishing an old order that had been disrupted by abuses of power and corruption but, rather, with the liberation and further moral development of humanity and with the founding of a political community which corresponded to the dictates of reason and morality. It lent an unmistakable flavor not only to the concept of revolution after 1789,[16] but also to the constitutions produced under its influence. It was this quality that Kant interpreted as a "historical sign."

After 1789, the term "revolution" took on the primary meaning of the overthrow of a political and social order by its subjects;[17] the older meaning of a recurring cycle of events that had been borrowed from astronomy and from Copernicus's work *De revolutionibus orbium coelestium* [*On the Orbits of Celestial Bodies*] of 1543 ceased to be applied to political circumstances. This was not yet the case in the earlier Glorious Revolution of 1688, which was regarded by the majority of contemporaries as a return to and restoration of a proper order that had merely been temporarily disturbed.[18] In the course of the Revolution of 1789, however, the neutral concept of revolution as rotation came to be connected with mass uprisings, civil war, and human progress toward the final design of Providence.[19] The term "revolution" acquired new and dynamic connotations of space, time, and content:[20] The entire world ought to profit from the gains of a revolution, which thus became global according to its own inner logic; this in turn implies that the state of revolution becomes permanent, since nothing suggests that its grandiose mission will ever be fulfilled in reality. The fear of an "*état continuel de révolution*" [a continual state of revolution] was expressed in the French National Assembly,[21] and this fear was based on the inherent tendency of a revolution to move from the political to the social sphere. One of the fundamental lessons of the French Revolution was that the success of a political revolution depends on the ability to pave the way by creating the right social conditions.

Hannah Arendt has pointed out that the centuries-old notion of cyclical recurrence of the various forms of government was based upon a distinction between rich and poor assumed to be natural and inevitable; it was the knowledge of the considerable prosperity existing in America that inspired the social dimension of the French Revolution. It appeared more important to revolutionaries to "change the fabric of society as it had been changed in America prior to its Revolution, than to change the structure of the political realm."[22] The success of the American Revolution, Arendt argues, was based on the fact that while there was poverty in America, there was no widespread misery such as existed in Europe; as a result the American revolutionaries could concern themselves with establishing a new form of government rather than transforming society.[23] This explains to a considerable extent the different outcomes of the American and French revolutions. The fact that the French Revolution, which ended in disaster, "has made world history" while the "triumphantly successful" American Revolution "has remained an event of little more than local importance"[24] is probably due in fact to the fateful but inevitable expansion of the political revolution in France to the social sphere. The Age of Enlightenment had done nothing to alter the fact that France, although considered the richest nation in Europe, was just as vulnerable as its neighbors to unpredictable food shortages:

> The government, at all levels, worried about food supply as earnestly as the consumers. Subsistence was the chief common interest which attached them to each other; their shared anxiety to deal successfully with the subsistence problem served as a sort of mutual guarantee of fidelity and responsibility.[25]

No matter whether the modern absolutist state felt threatened by indirect powers, literary circles, secret philosophical societies, or religious sects,[26] or whether the newly emerging bourgeoisie felt challenged by new taxes, in the words of a French contemporary, the ability of the *ancien régime* to maintain itself depended in the last analysis on its ability "to provide for the subsistence of the people, without which there is neither law nor force which can contain them."[27] As Kaplan's study shows, the connection between bread and politics was plainly apparent to the representatives of the *ancien régime*, even if politics still took the form of typical absolutist policy. But if satisfying the basic needs of the population was a task for policy, then a revolutionary transformation of the entire political order necessarily had to seize this motive for order and connect it with the idea of moral progress. The connecting link became the principle of popular sovereignty.

The proclamation of popular sovereignty by the French National Assembly meant far more than merely transferring the legitimate exercise of supreme power to the people, that is, denying all other claims to the right to rule, be it by a monarch, a hereditary aristocracy, or an intellectual or propertied elite.[28] This was without precedent in Europe, although the Americans had proceeded under similar, if more favorable, conditions. In France the claim was raised and enforced that the sovereign will of the people is nothing less than the fount and standard of earthly justice and the agency for fulfilling the dictates of historical reason. In contrast to the American Revolution inspired by the teachings of John Locke, the political theory of the French Revolution saw no limits on sovereignty imposed by natural law, and thus the sovereign nation becomes godlike, the personification of its own history. "The manner in which a nation exercises its will does not matter," declared Abbé Sieyès on the eve of the Revolution, "the point is that it does exercise it; any procedure is adequate, and its will is always the supreme law."[29] After the abolition of the monarchy, the people were substituted for the nation, and the Revolution, which had begun with the rebellion of the nobility against the monarchy and had quickly assumed the character of a revolution of the Third Estate against the *ancien régime*,[30] could take the form of a permanent social revolution; now there was no ideal for the people to strive for except their own (material) well-being.

The theoretical foundation for thus combining the idea of public or popular welfare (accepted by absolutist rulers) with that of rule based on the assent of the ruled (which went back to the Middle Ages)[31] had been provided in 1762 by Rousseau in *The Social Contract*. Rousseau himself was anything but a social revolutionary, however; paradoxically, he wanted to use his concept of the "seemingly revolutionary form of the republic (popular sovereignty) to preserve traditional social conditions doomed to extinction,"[32] although it was then precisely this revolutionary political form that later unleashed the social revolution. The theoretical impact and momentous effect of his rationale for popular sovereignty were based on the fact that he stripped the notion of the whole over which rule is exercised, which is essential for the justification of rule, of all social characteristics and constructed it following the model of the individual in natural law as a collective person furnished with unrestricted power and endowed with a will. We find this thought expressed in particularly radical form by his most loyal (if slightly eccentric) pupil, Sieyès:

> We must conceive the nations of the world as being like men living outside society or "in a state of nature," as it is called. . . . To imagine a legitimate society, we assumed that the purely natural *individual* will had enough moral power to form the association; how then can we refuse to recognize a similar power in the equally natural *common* will?[33]

In Hobbes's and Locke's theories of the social contract, individuals had transferred—albeit in different ways—the power they possessed in a state of nature to a third party, who thereby became entitled to rule over them.[34] While in Hobbes's theory each individual of a group enters into a contract with every other individual with the aim of having themselves embodied by a third party, and the group achieves unity only in and through his person,[35] in Rousseau's system the individuals themselves form an association through the social contract, an "artificial and collective body, . . . and by this same act that body acquires . . . its common *ego*, its life and its will."[36] The individuals now associated in a unit thereby become their own sovereign. It is logically impossible for any obligations to be imposed on the sovereign, however. The sovereign is "in the position of a private person making a contract with himself,"[37] and as a result his will as expressed in law cannot be unjust, "because no one is unjust to himself."[38] This is the solution to the riddle of "how we can be both free and subject to laws"[39] — namely, that "each individual, while uniting himself with the others, obeys no one but himself."[40] This construction of a sovereign without subjects created a theoretical problem of which Rousseau was certainly aware, although its full consequences would not manifest themselves until the twentieth century.[41] This was the potential contradiction between the omnipotence of the popular will and the possible empirical limitations of its wisdom.

As we saw above, Hobbes had resolved this contradiction for absolutist governments with the dictum *"autoritas, non veritas, facit legem"* ["authority, not truth, makes law"]. He had been concerned with protecting sovereign state power from competing claims of religious or philosophical truth; he was convinced that the state could guarantee internal peace only by drawing a line between truth and politics and imposing state rule. But through the Revolution society had defeated the sovereignty of the state and united its own universalist morality with the absolute power of the sovereign.[42] The idea of human progress had found a powerful and effective agent; of course, it had to carry the guarantee of its historical reason within itself, or at least possess the potential for showing itself to be reasonable. Both alternatives played a role in the French Revolution, and for both the question of a constitution was significant, although the accents were placed differently. The Constitution of 1791 still names the conditions of social progress by guaranteeing human rights and providing for the separation of powers; the Constitution of 1793 — which, significantly, never went into effect — is by contrast an instrument for increasing the power of the sovereign, who can achieve the goal mentioned in Article 1, of maintaining "the common welfare,"[43] only by ceaselessly striving to eliminate all obstacles in its way.

Thus the thought regarded as central to the modern constitutional state, namely, the limitation of government power,[44] did not play a central role in the French Revolution at all. Certainly it appears paradoxical, at least at first glance, to combine the principle of democracy with the idea of a constitution: The democratic revolution was concerned with establishing popular sovereignty and liberating a supreme will legitimized by itself and unlimited in earthly terms, after all, and a constitution seems to imply the binding, limitation, and even control of this supreme power. This contradiction becomes all the more acute if we associate the idea of popular sovereignty with the principle of the moral and social progress of humanity in general, as the Jacobin phase of the French Revolution tended to do, for what justification can there be for obstructing such a goal? If we observe the history of modern constitutionalism from its origins in the last quarter of the eighteenth century up to the present day, we can see that the true theme of democratic constitutionalism was hidden behind the superficial need to limit the power of the sovereign: Can we and should we assign to the democratic sovereign and his originally unlimited power the ability and mission to recognize historical reason and carry out its dictates?

Rousseau himself, the first person to formulate this question, was by no means convinced that the people would always will what was correct, and he resigned himself to the conclusion that a real democracy had thus never existed and never would.[45] Obviously the problem lay in the premise of the contract as he understood it: The collective person created by the contract cannot develop beyond a state of nature—in contrast to its individual members[46]—because it has no partner with whom to enter into possible obligations. While individuals are freed from the stupidity and narrowness of their natural existence through their participation in the social contract[47] and gain a legally ordered form of freedom, the full potential of their natural power and liberty is transferred to the collective person they have created, so that this person becomes, in a manner of speaking, an artificial natural creature. If the sovereign can will anything, even what is unreasonable, then his constitutionalization consists not in the limitation of his power and ability to will but, rather, solely in taking measures to ensure that what he wills is reasonable. It is for this reason that Sieyès, the most consistent advocate of this prelegal natural empowerment of the nation, deviated on a crucial point from Rousseau, who had made the well-known point that every form of delegation or representation of the will of the people is incompatible with popular sovereignty.[48] Sieyès, by contrast, stubbornly defended representative government. He concurred with his teacher that the nation is sovereign and not bound to any constitution, but he argued that sovereignty can only be exercised through the constituted power of a representative assembly, which offers the best guarantee that particular interests will not dominate the general consensus. Even the most basic power of a nation, the power to constitute itself, is exercised in Sieyès's version of the theory not by the people directly but by their representatives.[49] By distinguishing between the possession and exercise of sovereignty, Sieyès succeeded in reconciling popular sovereignty with constitutionalism. It is likely that he could successfully persuade the National Assembly to accept this compromise only because he saw a constitution not as a restriction but as an instrument that made political action possible.

For Sieyès the nation was still identical with the Third Estate, and as the Constitution of 1791 shows, its rule seemed to him quite compatible with a monarchical system of government. It is significant that Rousseau saw the ideal form of the state created by the social contract as a republic[50] and not a democracy, which is characterized by a union of the legislative and executive powers and thus represents "a government without government, so to speak."[51] And so, after the abolition of the monarchy on 21 September 1792, the nation was declared a republic, and Year 1 of the French Republic began the following day. As we have seen, Robespierre then identified the Republic with democracy in his speech of 5 February 1794 and he went on to speak of democracy as a state "where the sovereign people, guided by the laws which are its own work, does everything it can do itself, and has everything it cannot do itself performed by delegates."[52] Saint-Just, in his speech of 13 November 1792, had demanded the death sentence for the king in the name of the Republic,[53] but soon thereafter Robespierre demanded that laws should be promulgated in the name of the French people instead.[54] Article 61 of the Convention's Constitution of 1793 contained this change. Hannah Arendt has pointed out that from the beginning the Jacobins, at least, used the term "people" to mean the lower classes, the poor and wretched, and that compassion for their fate represented one of the forces driving the revolutionary process.[55] This had nothing to do yet with the socialist ideas of the nineteenth century, let alone with raising the poor and exploited to the subject of historical progress. For Robespierre it was obvious that "the extreme disproportion of wealth is the source of many evils and many crimes, but we are no less convinced that equal distribution of wealth is an illusion"; he concluded that "it is much more a question of making poverty honorable than of proscribing opulence."[56] Significantly, he added that an equal distribution of property "is necessary not so much for individual happiness as for the general welfare"—an echo of Rousseau's statement that "a large measure of equality in social rank and fortune" is a necessary condition for democracy.[57] Rousseau's idea that the people of a democracy are "already bound together by some original association, interest or agreement"[58] before any political union occurs was confirmed, materially speaking, by the shared misery of the masses who became caught up in the revolutionary movement. His description of a multitude driven by a single will "was an exact description of what they actually were, for what urged them on was the quest for bread, and the cry for bread will always be uttered with one voice."[59]

It was thus that the social question of the Revolution could be combined with the political and constitutional question of sovereignty. Since sovereignty was based on the natural unity and unrestricted freedom of will of the people, it was logical that their fundamental needs became paramount and that the Revolution would inevitably expand from the political to the social sphere. How very eloquent we find the "association of bread and law"[60] in the proclamation of the sansculottes of 20 May 1795. It is itself formulated in the language of a constitution and presents their basic demands in Article 1: "1. Bread. 2. The dismissal of the revolutionary government. 3. Immediate proclamation of the democratic constitution of 1793."[61] This constitution had, of course, embodied the principle of popular sovereignty (in the sense of direct rule of the empirical popular will with no intermediate agency) with particular consistency.[62] More than sixty years later, Alexis de Tocqueville would trace this social tendency of the Revolution back to the absolutist period in French history, when "the whole nation . . . wanted reforms rather than rights" and created an all-powerful central administration that proceeded to reorganize society long before the Revolution occurred:

> They had accepted as the ideal of a social order a people with no other aristocracy than that of public officials, a sole and omnipotent administrative director of the State and guardian of individuals. Though wishing to be free, they did not intend to depart from their original idea; they merely tried to reconcile it with that of liberty.[63]

Indeed, the political aims of the French Revolution grew to be directed ever more radically at relieving the misery and suffering of the masses instead of establishing lasting institutions,[64] and the enormous scope of this task meant continual delays in turning attention to a new constitution.[65] "A revolution is the war of liberty against its enemies; a constitution is the rule of victorious and peaceful liberty," Robespierre had proclaimed.[66] With this statement, four and a half years after 17 June 1789, he had reversed the relationship between constitution and revolution. The collapse of the *ancien régime* had begun with the Third Estate's transformation of itself into the National Assembly and the Tennis-Court Oath three days later not to disband until they had established a constitution for the realm; it was this act that unleashed the Revolution. But now it turned out that not only did a constitution not represent the culmination of the Revolution, it actually stood in the way of the Revolution's further progress. Robespierre's appeal—"we want to replace egoism with morality in our country, honor with probity, customs with principles, proprieties with duties, the tyranny of fashion with the empire of reason ... an amiable, frivolous and miserable people with a people magnanimous, powerful, and happy"[67]—is the program of a permanent revolution; it can never be concluded, for the establishment of a democracy continually provides new tasks and goals. "Since the soul of the Republic is virtue and equality," all political activity must be related "to maintaining equality and developing virtue."[68] If the "rule of liberty," a constitution, can only be put into effect after the enemies of liberty have been defeated, then liberty precedes the constitution and must have its guarantees outside the constitution—in the revolution and, in the last analysis, the virtue of the people. Here Robespierre planted the seed for a future development in which the idea of progress came to be detached from its original association with a constitution and linked with new and powerful historical forces.

If one takes the U.S. Constitution as a contrast, one could conclude that its longevity has resulted directly from its minimal ambitions to alter society. Although it, too, was the product of a revolution, it has proven remarkably viable and robust. Over a span of two hundred years characterized by immense social change and the development of the United States into a world power, it has been amended only twenty-six times (only fourteen times if the immediate addition of the Bill of Rights and the establishment and repeal of prohibition are not counted).[69] The reasons for this unique success story of a written constitution have been much debated;[70] there is considerable evidence to suggest that the most important reasons are to be sought less in the structure of the Constitution itself than in the geographic, social, cultural, and religious conditions that produced it. The difference between the basic concepts of the U.S. and first French constitutions is so significant, however, that it should probably be regarded as at least a contributing cause of the vastly different outcomes of the two revolutions.

Both revolutions claimed to have established popular sovereignty and an assembly to draft a constitution, an assembly that by definition is a nonconstituted power and therefore founded on direct democracy and the power of the people.[71] The fathers of the U.S. Constitution succeeded in assembling constitutional conventions that were viewed as particularly representational and democratic, and therefore legitimate; they also managed to bind the process of approving, amending, or abolishing the Constitution to rules mentioned in the Constitution itself,[72] thereby constitutionalizing the *pouvoir constituant* [constitutional power] (see Article 5 of the U.S. Constitution).[73] The French Constitution of 1791 contained provisions for amendments in Article 7, but the vote of the National Assembly of 11 August 1792 to call a National Convention did not follow this prescribed procedure. The members of the Assembly did not "have the right," they argued, "to subject the exercise of [popular] sovereignty to binding rules";[74] they even formulated their own decree as an invitation to the people to elect the delegates to the convention in the manner suggested, so that the convention itself acquired the status of a revolutionary rather than a constitutional convention.[75] While the Americans were familiar with the idea of a revolutionary convention from English history and the Glorious Revolution of 1688,[76] this recourse to the people had meant something different there than it did in revolutionary France. In the tradition of John Locke[77]—who, in contrast to Hobbes and Rousseau, considers a state of nature to have all the essential qualities of a society with property and contracts and therefore sees the purpose of the social contract as by no means solely to protect the basic needs of individuals[78]— the term "people" means not a collective person but, rather, "the endless variety of a multitude whose majesty resided in its very plurality."[79] The power of the people thus did not consist in the sum of "natural" powers of individuals living in a state of nature that had been transferred to an authority; instead, it took the form of a government whose authority was legally limited from the start and was received from individuals between whom obligations had previously existed and who had thus not created a government from a state of nature. The experiences of the American colonists with their many and varied compacts and covenants make it appear plausible that their first notion of a social contract would be that of an agreement among equals; through it they joined together in a community (in both a religious and a secular sense), overcoming their powerlessness as isolated individuals. The triumph over the state of nature is brought about by the security that the rule of law is expected to provide; the law thus antecedes the existence of a power able to guarantee its enforcement. And in turn this security under the rule of law is based on the mutual trust[80] of those who are engaged in a perilous common undertaking. Political power arises not from the "fictitious" consignment of the power of "aboriginal" individuals to a sovereign, but from the transfer of limited authority of an already legally constituted and reciprocal kind to a government.[81]

The notion of unconditional and unrestricted national or popular sovereignty was thus foreign to even the most radically republican antifederalists[82] in the newly independent United States—how much more so to the fathers of the U.S. Constitution, who viewed the hypothesis of a unified and rational collective will with extreme suspicion.[83] But their constitutional theories did not rely on such a hypothesis, since their aim was to create a public authority that would protect the liberty of citizens—and at the end of the eighteenth century this meant the liberty of property owners—most effectively. The idea that such a public authority might have a historical mission above and beyond the protection of the rights of individuals or that it embodied the higher reason of a single common will seemed not only foreign to them but a positive threat. For this reason they took particular care to fragment and scatter the opportunities for the people to express its will by popular vote.[84] In this way they hoped to eliminate the possibility of oppression of the property-owning minority by the propertyless majority. The desire to guarantee individual liberty is also reflected in the structure of the Constitution, in that it created no single center of public authority; instead, it left many powers to the states and divided the powers of the federal government, creating a system of checks and balances from which the idea of a single sovereign has been virtually eliminated. Thus we find a complete lack of the stirring appeals to the sovereignty of the people that have been associated in Europe with the notions of collective reason and social and moral progress since the French Revolution. Perhaps Hannah Arendt was correct in saying that the American revolutionaries acted in a land "into which the fearful spectacle of human misery, the haunting voices of abject poverty, never penetrated," and that when they spoke of reason ruling the passions, they understood passions as a form of irrationality requiring suppression rather than as a cry for bread and social justice.[85] In any case, however, to claim that popular sovereignty and constitutionalism are irreconcilable concepts[86] is to oversimplify the problem, since this ignores the constitutional tradition founded in the French Revolution. This tradition has had a lasting effect on constitutional thinking in Germany, even if it may appear to some as the "Jacobinism" of a "vulgarly democratic ideology."[87]

Notes

1. See P. Häberle, "1789 als Teil der Geschichte, Gegenwart, und Zukunft des Verfassungsstaates," in H. Krauß, ed., *Folgen der französischen Revolution* (Frankfurt, 1989), 61ff.
2. I. Kant, *Der Streit der Fakultäten*, in W. Weischedel, ed. *Werke* (Frankfurt, 1977), 11, 358 [my translation—DLS]. For more on Kant in relation to the French Revolution see H. Reinalter, *Die französische Revolution und Mitteleuropa* (Frankfurt, 1988), 185ff.
3. Ibid., 361.
4. See Hofmann, "Zur Idee des Staatsgrundgesetzes."
5. Cited according to Anderson, *Select Documents Illustrative of the History of France*, 61.
6. K. Loewenstein, *Volk und Parlament nach der Staatstheorie der französischen Nationalversammlng von 1789* (1922; reprint, Aalen, 1964), 126ff; see also H. Hofmann, "Zur Herkunft der Menschenrechtserklärungen," *Juristiche Schulung* 28 (1988): 841ff.
7. M. Robespierre, *Discours et rapports à la Convention* (Paris, 1965), 207–41; quote, 212–13 [here and in following quotations my translation—DLS].
8. W. Mager, "Republik," in O. Brunner et al., eds., *Geschichtliche Grundbegriffe* 5 (Stuttgart, 1984), 549ff, 589ff.
9. Ibid., 596–97.
10. See *The Federalist Papers*, ed. B. F. Wright (Cambridge, Mass., 1961), no. 10 (129–36), no. 14 (150–55), and no. 39 (280–86), all by James Madison.
11. Robespierre, *Discours et rapports*, 213.
12. Montesquieu, *The Spirit of Laws,* trans. T. Nugent (New York, 1949), bk. 3, sec. 3 (vol. 1, 20–22), and bk. 5, sec. 3, (vol. 1, 41–42).
13. Mager, "Republik," 596.
14. Robespierre, *Discours et rapports*, 216.
15. Ibid., 213.
16. For the reflection of the new awareness of time in literature see K. H. Bohrer, "Zeit der Revolution—Revolution der Zeit," *Merkur* 479, no. 1 (1989): 13ff.
17. For more on the concept of revolution see K. Griewank, *Der neuzeitliche Revolutionsbegriff: Entstehung und Entwicklung,* 2nd ed. (Frankfurt, 1969); H. Arendt, *On Revolution* (New York, 1963), 13ff; T. Schieder, "Revolution," in C. D. Kernig, ed., *Marxismus im Systemvergleich* 4 (Freiburg im Br., 1973); R. Koselleck et al., "Revolution, Rebellion, Aufruhr, Bürgerkrieg," in Brunner et al., eds., *Geschichtliche Grundbegriffe* 5; R. Koselleck, the chapter "Historische Kriterien des neuzeitlichen Revolutionsbegriffs," in R. Koselleck, ed., *Vergangene Zukunft: Zur Semantik geschichtlicher Zeiten* (Frankfurt, 1989), 67ff.
18. Griewank, *Der neuzeitliche Revolutionsbegriff*, 150; Arendt, *On Revolution*, 35–36.
19. Griewank, *Der neuzeitliche Revolutionsbegriff*, 187ff.
20. Koselleck, "Historische Kriterien des Revolutionsbegriffs," 76ff.
21. Cited by Loewenstein, *Volk und Parlament*, 292–93.

22. Arendt, *On Revolution*, 15–17; quote, 17.
23. Ibid., 62–63.
24. Ibid., 49.
25. S. L. Kaplan, *Bread, Politics, and Political Economy in the Reign of Louis XV* (The Hague, 1976), 1, xvii.
26. See R. Koselleck, *Kritik und Krise* (Freiburg and Munich, 1959), 49ff.
27. Kaplan, *Bread, Politics, and Political Economy*, 4.
28. E.-W. Böckenförde, "Demokratie als Verfassungsprinzip," in Isensee and Kirchhof, eds., *Handbuch des Staatsrechts* 1 (Heidelberg, 1987), 893, sec. 10.
29. E.-J. Sieyès, *What Is the Third Estate?*, trans. M. Blondel (New York, 1964), 128.
30. See G. Lefebvre, *The Coming of the French Revolution, 1789*, trans. R. R. Palmer (New York, 1957).
31. For more details see P. Graf Kielmansegg, *Volkssouveränität: Eine Untersuchung der Bedingungen demokratischer Legitimität* (Stuttgart, 1977), 16ff, 59ff; Q. Skinner, *The Foundations of Modern Political Thought* 2 (Cambridge, 1978), 161ff.
32. I. Fetscher, *Rosseaus politische Philosophie: Zur Geschichte des demokratischen Freiheitsbegriffs* (Neuwied, 1960), 257.
33. Sieyès, *What Is the Third Estate?*, 127–28.
34. See U. K. Preuss, *Politische Verantwortung und Bürgerloyalität: Von den Grenzen der Verfassung und des Gehorsams in der Demokratie* (Frankfurt, 1984), 66ff.
35. Hobbes, *Leviathan*, pt. 2, chs. 17 and 18, 223–39.
36. Rousseau, *The Social Contract*, bk. 1, ch. 6, 61.
37. Ibid., bk. 1, ch. 7, 62.
38. Ibid., bk. 2, ch. 6, 82.
39. Ibid.
40. Ibid., bk. 1, ch. 6, 60.
41. Ibid., bk. 2, ch. 3, and bk. 3, ch. 4.
42. See Koselleck, *Kritik und Krise*, 132ff.
43. Cited according to Anderson, ed., *Select Documents Illustrative of the History of France*, 171.
44. C. H. McIlwain, *Constitutionalism Ancient and Modern*, 2nd ed. (Ithaca, N.Y., 1947), 21–22; C. J. Friedrich, *Der Verfassungsstaat der Neuzeit* (Berlin, 1953), 135ff and elsewhere.
45. Rousseau, *The Social Contract*, bk. 3, ch. 4, 112.
46. Ibid., bk. 1, ch. 8, 65.
47. Ibid.
48. Ibid., bk. 3, ch. 15, 141.
49. Sieyès, *What Is the Third Estate?*, 130; for details see E. Zweig, *Die Lehre vom pouvoir constituant: Ein Beitrag zum Staatsrecht der französischen Revolution* (Tübingen, 1909), 118ff; Redslob, *Die Staatstheorien der französischen Nationalversammlung*; Loewenstein, *Volk und Parlament*, 3ff.
50. Rousseau, *The Social Contract*, bk. 1, ch. 6, 61; see also bk. 2, chs. 8–10.
51. Ibid., bk. 3, ch. 4, 112.

52. Robespierre, *Discours et rapports*, 214.
53. Saint-Just, *Discours et rapports*, ed. Albert Soboul (Paris, 1957), 62–69.
54. Cited according to J. M. Thompson, *Robespierre* (Oxford, 1939), 339 and 365.
55. Arendt, *On Revolution*, 65ff, 69ff; see also the discussion of the word *"peuple"* in J. M. Thompson, *The French Revolution*, 2nd ed. (1944; reprint, Oxford, 1989), viii.
56. Speech of 24 April 1793; Robespierre, *Discours et rapports*, 177–18.
57. Rousseau, *The Social Contract*, bk. 3, ch. 4, 113.
58. Ibid., bk. 2, ch. 10, 95.
59. Arendt, *On Revolution*, 89; for more on the motive of hunger and its political significance see S. L. Kaplan, *The Famine Plot Persuasion in Eighteenth-Century France*, Transactions of the American Philosophical Society 72, part 3 (Philadelphia, 1982).
60. Zweig, *Die Lehre vom pouvoir constituant*, 401.
61. Buchez-Roux, *Histoire parlementaire de la Revolution francaise*, 40 vols. (Paris, 1834–1838), 36: 315–18.
62. See Kielmansegg, *Volkssouveränität*, 162–63.
63. A. d. Tocqueville, *The Ancien Régime*, trans. M. W. Patterson (Oxford, 1952), bk. 3, ch. 3, 174 and 176.
64. Arendt, *On Revolution*, 87.
65. For more on how the revolution influenced the structure of the French government see T. Skocpol, *States and Social Revolutions: A Comparative Analysis of France, Russia, and China* (Cambridge, 1979), 174ff.
66. M. Robespierre, in his speech of 25 December 1793 "On the Principles of Revolutionary Government," *Discours et rapports*, 190.
67. Robespierre, *Discours et rapports*, 212.
68. Ibid., 216.
69. See H. Vorländer, "Forum Amerikanum: Kontinuität und Legitimität der Vereinigten Staaten von Amerika," *Jahrbuch des öffentlichen Rechts der Gegenwart* 36 (1987): 542. [Vorländer subtracts 12 from 26 and comes up with 12; presumably his arithmetic was faulty, and he meant 14— DLS.]
70. For details see Vorländer, ibid. and the literature he cites.
71. For the American debates on sovereignty see Wood, *The Creation of the American Republic*, 334–54 and 532–43; for the constitutional implications of the term "constitution–giving power" see E.-W. Böckenförde, *Die verfassunggebende Gewalt des Volkes: Ein Grenzbegriff des Verfassungsrechts* (Frankfurt, 1986).
72. See Wood, *The Creation of the American Republic*, 306–43; Zweig, *Die Lehre vom pouvoir constituant*, 59ff; Loewenstein, *Volk und Parlament*, 87–88.
73. For details see Zweig, *Die Lehre vom pouvoir constituant*, 50ff, and for the corresponding French debates passim.
74. The decree is printed in J. Duvergier, ed., *Collection complète des lois, décrets, etc. de la France* 4 (Paris, 1834), 297.
75. For details see Zweig, *Die Lehre vom pouvoir constituant*, 324ff, 330–31.
76. Wood, *The Creation of the American Republic*, 318–19.

77. See the discussion in J. P. Young, "Amerikanisches politisches Denken: Von der Revolution bis zum Bürgerkrieg," in I. Fetscher and H. Münkler, eds., *Pipers Handbuch der politischen Ideen* 3 (Munich and Zurich, 1985), 617ff; see also Wood, *The Creation of the American Republic*, 282–91.
78. See Preuss, *Politische Verantwortung*, 66ff.
79. Arendt, *On Revolution*, 88.
80. Ibid., 182.
81. Ibid., 169–72.
82. Wood, *The Creation of the American Republic*, 59–60; for more on their ideas see also Young, "Amerikanisches politisches Denken," 631–32.
83. See *The Federalist Papers*, no. 10, by Madison, 129–36.
84. For more on the role of private property in the U.S. Constitution see J. Nedelsky, "American Constitutionalism and the Paradox of Private Property," in Elster and Slagstad, eds., *Constitutionalism and Democracy*, 241–73.
85. Arendt, *On Revolution*, 90–91.
86. C. J. Friedrich, *Der Verfassungsstaat der Neuzeit* (Berlin, 1953), 18–19; M. Kriele, *Einführung in die Staatslehre* (Reinbek b. Hamburg, 1975), 224ff.
87. E. Fraenkel, *Deutschland und die westlichen Demokratien*, 4th ed. (Stuttgart, 1968), 59ff.

✧ 3 ✧

The Struggle for Sovereignty: The People and Progress

Constitutional questions continued to play a significant role in the political struggles of the nineteenth century, at least in countries such as Belgium, Italy, and Germany, where the bourgeoisie was still striving to create a national state. The idea of a constitution was no longer associated with the rhetoric of revolution and progress, however. This rhetoric became associated instead with the strivings of the Fourth Estate, which were not directed toward a constitution at all. The task of improving social conditions took priority over achieving a constitution, and in addition, the notion of progress acquired a new polemical accent. At the time of the French Revolution, "progress" represented a universal category, as the unarguably beneficial incarnation of reason itself; its opposite was all that was unreasonable, despotic, arbitrary, unjust, and inhuman, and associating these qualities with the status quo and the absolute feudal rulers who maintained it placed those in power in a morally untenable position.[1] Over the course of the nineteenth century the morally unambiguous connection between the ideas of progress, revolution, and a constitution was lost. To be sure, the idea of "reaction" won out as the still-asymmetric opposite of "progress," and "the forces of revolution showed a tendency to recognize the forces of reaction as their only worthy opponent, and vice versa."[2] But now it was far less clear where progress and retrogression were located in society. Led by a bureaucracy eager to implement reforms and bring about a revolution from the top down, the state appeared as a virtual pioneer of progress, at least in the economic sphere. In a paradoxical reversal of the situation in the French Revolution, social and economic reform could be more radical in Prussia than elsewhere in Germany because "the willingness of the bureaucracy to initiate reform was not curbed by a constitution or a representative assembly."[3] In fact, the reformers did

59

have a clear notion of the connection between progress and a constitution, but it had nothing to do with either American or French ideas.
The famous Riga Memorandum written in 1807 by Karl Freiherr von
Altenstein, a leading exponent of reform in the Prussian bureaucracy,
contains numerous suggestions for restoring the prestige and vigor of
the defeated Prussian state; they include recommendations to try to
conceal the "financial embarrassment of the government" and to use
travelers and authors as informants and propagandists. Even bribery
was not to be ruled out, wrote Altenstein, whereby the rule should be
"to bribe liberally. . . . Small bribes are easily outmatched and thus a
waste of money."[4] Altenstein takes up the question of a constitution
with equal candor, but he uses the term in the old, prerevolutionary
sense of "the condition of the state as a whole." As a result the link
between the notions of progress and a constitution remains vague and
limited to appeals to the *zeitgeist*—and this at a time when the modernization of society through the medium of a written and normative
constitution seemed essential.

> If the *zeitgeist* or the sum of human progress to a higher goal intervenes
> and exerts a powerful influence from within or without and alters the
> state of things . . . , then a constitution becomes altered automatically,
> if it has not been placed under fetters that make this impossible. To
> loosen such bonds is the duty of the supreme authority in the state.
> Alteration of the fundamental constitution is merely yielding to the
> demands of the *zeitgeist*. . . . The highest ideal of a constitution is to
> have its every provision not just make progress possible, but require it.[5]

What Altenstein is proposing here is an end to feudal society, and,
with what clearly seemed to him advisable caution, he himself suggests
"a form of national representation" on the basis of limited male suffrage. The point of all this, however, is to promote "a connection
between the nation and the state administration." The constitution's
aim is "to bind the nation to the administration and thereby acquire
control of all its power."[6] This corresponded to conditions in Germany at the beginning of the nineteenth century; the state and its administration were the main proponents of social reform—that is, progress,
but progress now had only a loose connection at best to the idea of
universal human rights and none whatsoever to the democratic foundations of the American and French constitutions. "Progress" meant
the elimination of the feudal fetters that were inhibiting the growth of
a nation-state, but the driving force behind progress and the medium

through which it was to be brought about were not free individuals and their political organizations but the state, which is antecedent to such organizations and exists in its own right. There is no intrinsic link between progress and a constitution, not only because progress is possible without a constitution (since the state's true "constitution" is the "condition" of the administration), but also because the moral implications of the idea of progress, human self-improvement, and the higher development of humanity as a whole have been lost.

Since the two revolutions of the eighteenth century, progress as a political category had become inseparable from the natural freedom of individual and collective self-determination, and a constitution that did not embody this principle could not claim to be progressive. Since a constitution is itself an expression of freedom, it could only come into existence in an act of freedom, a revolution of liberation. Thus the author of the article "Legal Progress" in the *Staats-Lexikon* of Rotteck and Welcker, the bible of German liberals in the period preceding the March revolution of 1848, after asking "whether and to what extent a revolution can possibly emanate from the principle of thraldom [nonfreedom] or the ruling feudal authority itself, that is, whether a revolution can be legal," came to the following conclusion:

> [It is] difficult to reconcile with the notion of freedom. Perfect freedom is essentially the result of an internal process, a product of organic development, and as such can never be merely grafted onto a person or a people from without.... As long as a people is asking or hoping for freedom, that is, a part of its own nature, from an external power, it is not free; it would make a mockery of all human logic to say that an external decree could grant a people the right to be free, that is to say, human.[7]

Despite all the "concessions [made by] the feudal state authority," according to this argument it had only two alternatives: "either to return to pure absolute rule and the principle of thraldom, or to go forward to the principle of pure democracy."[8] Arnold Ruge, a leftist Hegelian who was an associate of Karl Marx until 1844 and a left-wing delegate to the National Assembly in Frankfurt in 1848, expressed the same view in even more radical terms:

> Reaction ... is the revolution reversed, the counterrevolution.... Revolution and reaction are both the offspring of theory, only with the difference that one has truth and the other caprice as its content.... Both find their path blocked by the political present in the form of

laws and constitutions, and so both abstract from or break the law,
reaction in favor of the past . . . the revolution in favor of the future. But the future is unavoidable.[9]

Prussia still had no constitution at that time, that is, it had still not performed that "act of the general will," in the words of Immanuel Kant, "through
which the masses become a people,"[10] and the bureaucratic elites had lost
their enthusiasm for reform in the stifling atmosphere of the age of
restoration following Napoleon's defeat. The monarchs of most other
German states had either granted constitutions unilaterally or negoti-
ated them with representatives of the citizenry; these constitutions placed
limits on the monarch's powers[11] but were not based on popular sovereignty, and although they included certain basic rights, these were
not seen as the origin and standard legitimizing political authority.[12]
Instead, these rights represented enclaves of private freedom within a
society ruled by the monarch and his bureaucrats with limited participation granted to elected representatives of the propertied and educated bourgeoisie. In a strange form of pleonasm they were called
konstitutionelle Verfassungen in German [constitutional constitutions],
since in this instance *Verfassung* meant nothing more than the existing
form of rule, to which the written constitution now gave formal, legal
recognition. Johann Christian Majer had expressed this point of view
quite frankly in his *Allgemeine Theorie der Staatskonstitution* [*General Theory
of State Constitutions*] of 1799, when he defined "constitution" as the "status quo."[13] In the period leading up to the revolution of 1848, this status
quo was hovering indecisively between monarchical and popular sovereignty,
and it was this unsettled question that Arnold Ruge (still a radical at that
time) had in mind when he wrote that "the political present in the form of
laws and constitutions" was standing in the way of both revolution and
counterrevolution. For the liberals of the period only a democratic constitution could put an end to this stagnation, and they were prepared to accept a
revolution to achieve one if necessary, just as the author of the article on
"Constitutions" in the Brockhaus Encyclopedia had sensed as early as 1830:
The people, he wrote, "feel a vague urge to alter their present state, and the
idea from which they hope for alleviation of their complaints presents itself
to them currently in the guise of a constitution."[14] Here the term "constitution" was synonymous with popular sovereignty and freedom, and in turn
these were seen as guarantees of progress. When it came time to swear the
revolutionary oath in 1848, however, it soon became evident that the terms
were not so identical after all. Within the National Assembly, which was

meeting in St. Paul's Church in Frankfurt to draft a democratic national constitution, various factions soon emerged urging different versions of a "democratic monarchy,"[15] similar to the French National Assembly of 1791. Not all the delegates, it turned out, were willing to equate popular sovereignty with progress. After the assembly's constitution was rejected, the German bourgeoisie gave the issue of national unity priority over democracy in the following decades, since it did not appear possible to attain both simultaneously. At the same time the idea of progress became associated less with politics and more and more with the economic and industrial sphere, so that the torch of democratic progress was passed to new social forces and their intellectual heralds. It would soon transpire, however, that in their case as well the idea of progress would increasingly lose its connection with that of a constitution, largely because of an ambiguous definition of "democracy."

Karl Marx, of whom we must naturally speak here, was not willing to confine himself to more or less dark hints about the power of the future and the close affinity of revolution and truth, as Arnold Ruge had been. In his "Contribution to the Critique of Hegel's Philosophy of Law" he expressed the opinion—still shared by the radical democrats among the bourgeoisie—that a constitution must be a "genuine expression of the popular will," "if man is to do consciously what otherwise he is forced to do without consciousness by the nature of the thing." Therefore it becomes necessary, Marx continued, that "the movement of the constitution, that *advance* [progress], be made the *principle of the constitution* and that therefore the real bearer of the constitution, the people, be made the principle of the constitution. Advance itself is then the constitution."[16]

This somewhat mysterious sentence signals a highly significant shift of direction, where Marx's path diverges from that of the radical democrats. The latter accepted the equation "democratic constitution = progress," because the fact that all men were created equally free by nature meant that excluding the majority of the members of society—the people in the sense of the masses—from the political decision-making process would be completely contrary to reason. Thus the constitutional progress achieved in the course of the past—and it is almost universally accepted that such progress has occurred—has taken the form of giving more and more citizens the right to vote: from the elimination of property ownership as a requirement to granting women's suffrage to lowering the minimum voting age.[17] The connection between progress and democracy thus consisted in the removal of more and more of the barriers keeping citizens from participating in the political process: Since democracy meant an increase in political freedom, it was therefore progress. If in the preceding discussions "popular constitutional government" was regarded as the epitome of progress, this was not meant to imply that "the people" had any special qualities or characteristics that gave them a particular affinity with progress. But this is precisely the direction in which Marx shifted the relationship between progress and democracy. If making "the people" into "the principle of the constitution" means that "progress itself" becomes "the constitution," then the progress does not lie in the fact that the people can now freely determine their own political destiny but, rather, in the fact that "the people" are the living embodiment of the idea of progress. Thus in a democracy, progress itself comes to power, through the people. According to Marx, two conditions must be fulfilled for the equation "democracy = progress" to be correct: The people must be made the principle of the constitution, and the people must have qualities which make them the representatives of progress. In Marx's view, this second condition was not fulfilled within the framework of bourgeois democracy, which he labeled as "merely political." Bourgeois democracies were based on the fact "that part of civil society emancipates itself and attains general domination; on the fact that a definite class, proceeding from its particular situation, undertakes the general emancipation of society. This class emancipates the whole of society but only provided that the whole of society is in the same situation as this class."[18]

This does not meet the criteria of "progress," however, because its aim is to liberate society as a whole and, in the last analysis, all mankind.[19] In the French Revolution it was Antoine-Nicolas de Condorcet above all who universalized the idea of progress by relating it "to the future condition of the human race." By this he understood "the abolition of inequality between nations, the progress of equality within each nation, and the true perfection of mankind."[20] Humanity or the human race were not themselves representatives of progress, however, but rather the objects of a process of self-perfection, so that Condorcet knew of no agent who would bring progress to humanity and whose rule would be nothing less than the final liberation of all humanity. There had been a few attempts before Marx to assign a privileged role to certain groups or social classes in achieving progress,[21] but none had linked universal progress with the claim that a universal social agent existed for achieving human perfection. Marx's groundbreaking theoretical in-

novation was twofold: First, he identified "the people"—a legal constitutional category meaning the political unity of a group or mass of
individuals—with a single social class, the proletariat; and second, he
declared that this class represented the interests of all of humanity in
progress, so that a democratic constitution is not progressive because
the people rule themselves but because the people are the subject of
progress. Let us quote the famous passage from Marx's introduction
to the *Critique of Hegel's Philosophy of Law:*

> Where, then, is the *positive* possibility of a German emancipation?
> Answer: In the formation of a class with *radical chains*, a class of civil
> society which is not a class of civil society, an estate which is the
> dissolution of all estates, a sphere which has a universal character by
> its universal suffering and claims no *particular right* because no *par-*
> *ticular wrong* but *wrong generally* is perpetrated against it; which can
> no longer invoke a *historical* but only a *human* title; which does not
> stand in any one-sided antithesis to the consequences but in an all-
> round antithesis to the premises of the German state; a sphere, finally,
> which cannot emancipate itself without emancipating itself from all
> other spheres of society and thereby emancipating all other spheres of
> society, which, in a word, is the *complete* loss of man and hence can
> win itself only through the *complete rewinning of man*. This dissolu-
> tion of society as a particular estate is the *proletariat*.[22]

Here Marx's dictum that "advance [progress] itself is the constitution,"
which appears somewhat puzzling on first glace, becomes clearer: Humanity's
interest in progress is embodied in a "universal class" whose interest in
emancipation is not limited or particular, since it is identical with the interests
of humanity as a whole. If this class is made the principle of the constitution and attains political power, then it is neither a class nor a particular interest that is in power but progress itself. However, it also
becomes clear that this theory is invalid on several grounds and oblit-
erates the connection between progress and democracy. To begin with:
Even if the interests of the universal class are identical with those of
humanity and it can thus exercise its rule in the name of humanity, it
can still not be "the people" in the sense meant in a theory of constitutional democracy, because there "people," as the body of all the
inhabitants of a circumscribed territory, is a collective subject characterized by its distinction from other "peoples." Marx's logic would
require us to assume that the interests of all these other peoples are
also identical with those of all humanity (and thus also those of the
universal class); this would lead, however, to the paradoxical result

that different peoples would all be represented in their various constitutions by "humanity" (in vulgar parlance, by the universal class and its representatives) and would thus lose their political existence as a "people." The universal class as the representative of the universal interests of humanity would always overpower the political unity of "the people" established by its constitution, in order to transcend its particularity; taken to extremes, the logic would even require that "the people" be dissolved and returned to its preconstitutional position, in which the interests of all human beings are the same: a state of nature.

The connection established in the last quarter of the eighteenth century between progress, popular sovereignty, and constitutional government consisted in the fact that a constitution gave citizens the formal means by which to constitute themselves as an entity in the medium of their natural freedom and to create an order through which they could either direct the process of social change driven mainly by the principles of individual freedom and pursuit of one's own interests (in the American version) or alter society by way of collective decisions (the main tendency of the French version). In other words, democratic constitutions enabled *the people* to rule *themselves* (including the risk of mistakes and errors), and it was progressive only because the fetters by which the people had previously been kept bound were broken and replaced by self-determination, not because the people had any inherent or privileged knowledge of what constitutes progress. If progress now becomes the constitution, as Marx claimed, then it becomes the subject of history, and from then on in a democracy there are two subjects competing for power: progress and the people. Then all that is needed is one determined and perhaps unscrupulous agent who wishes to carry out the historical mission of progress for the latent tension to be transformed into open struggle. This "progressive democracy" is thus a permanent, more or less open state of warfare between progress and the people for sovereignty. It is a struggle which a democratic constitution was supposed to end for all time.

And finally, history certainly offers examples in which a group qualified by particular characteristics was seen to have the right to represent a valuable idea and to rule in its name. This is the case with the Roman Catholic hierarchy; it was the principle of Edmund Burke's "virtual representation," and the limited franchise of eighteenth- and nineteenth-century bourgeois parliamentarism was based on the principle that a minority is qualified to be the exclusive representatives of the whole. In all these cases the mandate to govern is not based on election by the governed. So, too, the universal class of the proletariat represents not humanity but its interests in emancipation and progress, and its claim to govern is not based on its having been elected by humanity. The Americans may have had good reason for demanding "no taxation without representation," but the slogan "no emancipation without representation" would obviously be absurd, since one's interest in emancipation cannot be represented by someone else, and so there is no need for legal instruments and procedures through which humanity could delegate it—while, on the other hand, the right to decide one's own fate is the characteristic basis of democracy. From whatever standpoint one may view the matter, the universal class cannot be constitutionalized by a democratic constitution. It cannot become the people—and thus the vehicle of a necessarily particular rule—without betraying its universal task; but if, on the other hand, it claims political power, then it is no longer the people in the sense of a democratic constitution, and its rule cannot be democratically legitimized. It is accurate according to this concept that "the proletariat has no fatherland" because its real existence—one difficult one to grasp, admittedly—is only as the vehicle of the idea of universal progress; this led to the tragic result that in every country where representatives of the universal class tried to carry out its historic mission, they tended to be seen as usurpers rather than as liberators. Perhaps it was for this reason above all that these representatives allowed themselves to be compensated all the more lavishly with material goods. Thus the most radical linking imaginable between progress and constitutionalism led in fact to the severing of this connection. Marx was right on one point, however: The formation of a proletariat plunged constitutional optimism into a profound crisis, something he recognized better than anyone else.

There is thus a certain internal logic in the temporary breakdown in Germany a few years later—after the failure of the revolution of 1848—of the tradition founded in the French Revolution of a close connection between the ideas of revolution, progress, and a constitution. From now on each of these ideas goes its own way, developing independently of the others. After Bismarck succeeded in creating a German nation-state in the form of a monarchy, the bourgeoisie lost all interest in a constitution; furthermore, the tie between the national and constitutional questions that was characteristic of 1848 was finally cut for good, since the nation-state had been created against the democratic demands of the constitutional movement of 1848. And while the idea of progress had lost none of its universality, it now got caught in the cross fire of the class war that was breaking out, in which each side could claim, with some justice, to be its historically legitimate vehicle. The capitalist class could point to the basic conditions of all production, according to which material and intellectual progress was possible only if a portion of the wealth created was withheld from direct consumption—thereby exploiting the workers—and reinvested to increase productivity. In this sense capitalists appear "as the vehicle of universal interests," since "demands of any group to improve its present life conditions are inimical to the future interests of the entire society, and this trade-off between the present and the future is institutionalized as the conflict between wages and profit."[23]

The class of salaried workers is thus inevitably put in the position of the class which—to paraphrase Marx—truly claims a special right only because a particular wrong has been committed against it. But the working class also had good grounds for proclaiming itself to be the vehicle of progress, when they took the axiom of natural law that every individual was equally free and applied it to the sphere of material standards of living. This gave a new and negative significance to the term "people": The people are all those members of society "who are *not* distinguished and singled out on some grounds, who are *not* privileged, *not* raised above others through property, social status, or education," in short, the people are the proletariat.[24] If, as we have seen, progress demanded democracy, that is, the participation of the people in political rule, then it was only consistent from a constitutional standpoint to claim that the political power of the proletariat was true democracy, as long as the identification of the proletariat with the people was plausible; there was then no need of Marxist theory, according to which the proletariat, by virtue of its social position, represented the interest of mankind in progress for philosophical reasons. We shall return to this point later. For now I will just note that in the following epoch the communist and the radical socialist branch of the workers' movement used both arguments without always distinguishing clearly between them, in order to claim political power in the name of progress: as the subject of the interest of all mankind in emancipation and progress and as the embodiment of "the people" in the sense of all those excluded from the benefits of society—in short, both as humanity and as the people.

The notion that a constitution can serve as a medium for progress appears once more, briefly, in Germany in the Weimar Constitution of 11 August 1919; this constitution owed its unfortunate end less to its own insufficiencies than to the intensity of the social conflicts to which other constitutions would presumably also have succumbed, despite the praise later lavished on their unique quality.[25] The aim of the Weimar Constitution is expressed in the Preamble as "to further social progress," but in a mass democracy characterized by deep class and ideological divisions, the meaning of this phrase had become ambiguous. The constitution was a compromise between widely diverse and opposing factions in society, and in the crisis which followed in the early 1930s the substance and finally the legitimacy of such a compromise was challenged by both the far Right and the far Left.[26] Only a few political and constitutional theorists, most of them Social Democrats, recognized in this admittedly precarious compromise what was presumably Germany's only chance to have an independent democratic government under the existing conditions of extreme social antagonism; their hope was that class conflict could be limited to and resolved within the civilized provisions of an institutionalized competitive democracy. If this constitution furthered social progress, then it was by pointing out to the working class, which from a Social Democratic viewpoint was genuinely progressive, a means by which they could carry socialism to victory without a revolution. On the anniversary of the adoption of the Weimar Constitution in 1930, Hermann Heller, the most important constitutional theorist among the Social Democrats and a man whose ideas have remained influential to the present day, defended it both against Bolshevik dictatorship, which would mean "an unrestrained and lawless struggle, a chaos destructive of all culture," and against "fascist dictatorship," which would put "a violent halt to progressive developments in the future"; in his eyes there was no available alternative to the existing constitution, since it alone provided for progress in an orderly and civilized manner: "We call . . . the present constitution good, since it has the historically necessary form to force the inevitable social struggle to take civilized forms while it gives creative forces the freedom to design a better future."[27]

These remarks were aimed, on the one hand, at winning over the middle classes, whose coolness toward the Weimar Constitution was threatening to turn into a withdrawal from the class compromise which they embodied (and this is in fact what happened in 1933); on the other hand, Heller was also addressing those who, in view of the miserable conditions of the working class and the hardly more encouraging political tactics of the Social Democrats, had given up all hope of bringing about the kind of social progress called for in the constitution's Preamble *with* the constitution as opposed to *against* it. As the

collapse of the Weimar Republic appeared imminent, a peculiar combination of social and constitutional questions emerged, in which the
idea of social progress no longer put pressure on the constitution, as
had occurred in the previous history of the workers' movement, but
rather the reverse: The constitution became the last bastion for the
political existence of the workers' movement and thus for the legitimate presence of the social question in the constitution. We find this
thought expressed with crystal clarity by Ernst Fraenkel; beginning in
the late 1920s he was legal counsel to the Metal Workers' Union and
later also a legal advisor to the leadership of the German Social Democratic Party, so that he was confronted directly with the practical and
political consequences of the erosion of the Weimar Constitution, erosion which the Social Democrats were struggling desperately to stop.
According to Fraenkel, "dialectical democracy," the term he used for
the Weimar system, was "the form of the state in enlightened high
capitalism," in which the class opposition between capital and labor
was not overcome but was weakened enough so that despite this opposition a political consensus could be reached.[28]

In principle, Fraenkel's reference to the Weimar Constitution as "the
form of the state in high capitalism" is based on the theory of social
progress which predicts the phase of high capitalism will be followed
by late capitalism, and that in turn by socialism as the final step. But
in this transitional period the only goal is to preserve the constitutionally regulated relationship between the two opposing classes, and now
the constitution itself takes on a specific weight of its own with regard
to the ongoing historical process as a guarantor that the workers' movement will not be crushed. It becomes the last bulwark against the forces
of reaction. Such an interpretation of the constitution is in principle
quite conventional, based as it is on the progress-reaction polarity typical
of nineteenth-century thinking; here it acquires a new twist, however,
an interesting modification that will be of significance for the future,
in which one can perhaps recognize the first signs of Fraenkel's later
development into one of the most, if not the most, important exponents of the pluralist theory in Germany. Here for the first time we
encounter the notion that the irreconcilable conflicts of society need
not first be overcome and settled before political unity can be reached
in reality. If it is possible that "a people united in one nation retains
a minimum of common interests in its social life,"[29] and if these common interests are embodied in its constitution, then not only does a
safe space exist for public discussion of the remaining social conflicts,

but there is also a reversal of the Marxist doctrine quoted above, and *the constitution itself is progress.*

The idea is not yet fully developed, but the germ of it is there. Now it is not the fact *that* a constitution exists at all which constitutes progress, as in the wake of the revolutions of the eighteenth and nineteenth centuries; nor is the constitution's progressiveness based on the proclamation of social progress in the Preamble and the establishment of certain progressive social and political principles in the main text. The decisive point now is not any of the provisions contained in the constitution but, rather, the means provided to society by the very existence of the constitution to deal with its own irreconcilable divisions. The constitution represents a mode of self-government of which eighteenth- and nineteenth-century constitutions had no need, since class conflict had not yet reached the political sphere. Their progressiveness needed to go no further than the proclamation of freedom and universal human rights and the constitution of political power through the people. Not until the twentieth century did constitutions have to take the "class differences existing between their citizens"[30] into account as a political problem and solve it by providing for the coexistence of hostile social forces. However, the prepolitical conditions were entirely new. In the bourgeois revolutions it was possible to speak of the "natural freedom" of mankind, of its "natural" need to improve, and its "natural" ability to govern itself. But what unquestioned principles of order could be assumed in a society in which affiliation with a particular class and social group and their organizations mediated the relationship of individuals to the political sphere? The idea of a constitution which was greeted enthusiastically at the hour of its birth as the fulfillment of all hopes for political progress now becomes self-referential, since the conditions of its possible existence have become problematic. Its quality and social worth are measured not by the degree to which it establishes "eternal" and "true" principles as norms but by the institutions and procedures it provides for society to preserve its own existence in civilized form in the face of particularism and self-destructive tendencies. The intense discussions on the Weimar Constitution by each of the political camps are certainly an expression of the constitutional crisis of the time. But they also bear witness—quite apart from their intellectual level, which has not been reached again since— to the great theoretical advance represented by the discovery of the constitution's "reflexivity," that is, its ability to make its own existence possible, combined with the recognition that it was precisely herein that its contemporary political and moral progressiveness lay. The fact that after the war this "lesson of Weimar" led to a substantialization of the constitution and was turned into a concept of a "democracy able to defend itself" that derived from an authoritarian state[31] demonstrates how easily the lofty principle of constitutional reflexivity can fall victim to robust pressures from powerful social interest groups. However, its power lies in the fact that it can still criticize this perversion of the original intent of the constitution in the terms of the constitution itself—and not in the name of a social idea external to the constitution's own premises. Here I am running ahead of my argument, however, for it will emerge later that the concept of constitutional reflexivity is an unavoidable response, I believe, to certain quite specific social conditions which have developed only recently. Above all in socialist theory and practice, which were based entirely on the notion of progress, progress did not melt into the complex modes of democratic self-government, but retained a fixed address: the proletariat, which, as we have seen, had to play the difficult role of being universal and particular at the same time, namely, to represent both the totality of humankind and its interest in universal emancipation *and* "the people," that is, the exploited masses who had not yet been liberated. Since in the autumn of 1989 it was the people who brought down the government based on this concept, we should take a closer look at the inner logic of this process.

If the proletariat claims to represent both humanity and the people (in the sense of all those deprived of their rights), what are the consequences when it (or its party) comes to power, as happened after the 1917 Revolution in Russia and after World War II in Eastern Europe? Now those who had been deprived of their rights had suddenly become the rulers, and if they were not willing to acknowledge that from now on they were exercising authority in their own name and their own interests (an admission that would have been intellectually honest and consistent but morally questionable and out of tune with their own universalist dogma), then they were forced to declare that they were ruling in the interest of universal human emancipation. But now we encounter a paradox: It is precisely as a consequence of the theory which claimed to be the sole legitimate heir to the necessary unity between progress and democracy that the contrast between democracy and progress emerges. The rule of progress demands the rule of the proletariat, that is, the people in the above-mentioned negative sense; democracy is based on a more comprehensive definition of the term "people" as the sum of all the members of society inhabiting a circumscribed, politically constituted territory. The constitutional notion of "the people" is inclusive and defines the role of the citizen, while "the people" as the opposite of the property-owning, educated, and ruling class is exclusive and comes into conflict with the universalism of "people" as all citizens at the moment when it declares itself to be the "people" granted the right to rule by constitutional democracy. For then it must exclude from participation in political power all those who do not possess these identifying characteristics. That this is no mere theoretical conclusion but became political reality is demonstrated by the 1968–1974 constitution of the German Democratic Republic. It was amended to remove the statement of a classic democratic principle contained in Article 3 of the original constitution of 1949: "All government authority originates in the *people.*" This sentence was replaced by the declaration in Article 2, "All political power in the German Democratic Republic is exercised by the workers." Since the "class of cooperative farmers," the "members of the intelligentsia," and the "other strata of society" were thereby excluded from political rule, it was then necessary to declare them "allies of the working class" for them to be able to participate in the political process. This step represents a departure from the principle of equal freedom for all citizens of a society. From this it logically followed that the most notable constitutional form this principle had taken, one achieved only through protracted political struggle—the principle of "one man, one vote" and the equal weight of every vote that this implies—also had to be stricken from Article 3: Votes in the representative assembly, the *Volkskammer*, were distributed in advance to favor the Communist Party, an arrangement that the population was required to confirm periodically by acclamation.

Given this background, the chant of the crowds demonstrating in Leipzig, "We are the people," was more than just a protest against an unpopular government and also more than a collective rejection of the intolerable infiltration of all levels of society by the *Stasi* (secret police) and the blurring of all divisions between the government and the Communist Party. It was a rebellion directed not against the misuse of authority so much as against the very foundations of that authority. (We shall see later, however, that this purely theoretical deduction is overly simple and must be modified in view of the course taken by the 1989 revolution.) It can hardly be expressed more clearly than in the words of Karl Marx quoted above: It was the rebellion of that sphere of society

which has a universal character by its universal suffering and claims no *particular right* because no *particular wrong* but *wrong generally* is perpetrated against it; which can no longer invoke a *historical* but only a *human* title; which does not stand in any one-sided antithesis to the consequences but in an all-round antithesis to the premises of the German state; a sphere, finally, which cannot emancipate itself without . . . emancipating all other spheres of society.[32]

"We are the *people*" — this cry was first and foremost a reclaiming of the right to exercise power from the ruling party, a return to true democratic status, and the rejection of a claim to authority not based on the authentic will of the people, much as it might proclaim itself "in harmony with the processes of historical development."

This memorable phrase also permits a more far-reaching interpretation. "*We* are the people": This is reminiscent of the first sentence of the U.S. Constitution, "We the people of the United States," in which the subject is in the plural. In the American tradition the phrase "we the people" has the connotation of plurality and diversity, and if this heterogeneous group gives itself a constitution "to secure for ourselves and our posterity the blessing of freedom," then it is the forms of contractual exchange between different but free and equal individuals who constitute the commonwealth.[33] The cry "*We* are the people" should thus be understood not just as a defiant echo of the democratic principle according to which all government authority originates in the people; at the same time it is also the rejection of the suggestion contained therein that "the people" as the sovereign subject of political rule are the vehicle of a unified and collective will, which is valid merely by virtue of its existence, just as Carl Schmitt had postulated the "homogenous nature of the people" and declared (with an erroneous reference to Rousseau) that "what the people will is always good."[34]

In actual fact traditional European ideas of sovereignty resolved the tension and competition between the rule of reason and the rule of popular will in the idea of progress only temporarily. As we saw above, Hobbes had answered the question of whether laws are binding because they are just and reasonable or because they are based on the will of the sovereign with the laconic sentence: *Autoritas, non veritas, facit legem.* His model of rule is based on the opposition between *ratio* [reason] and *voluntas* [will]. Rousseau's construction of the social contract was able to overcome this opposition only in theory, by basing the inherent reason of the general will on the claim that all citizens will want only what is reasonable. In other words, they participate in forming the *volonté générale* [general will] not in their capacity as *bourgeois*, but as *citoyens*. Rousseau held that "*Voluntas rationalis facit legem*" [rational will makes the law]—although he realized at the same time that this condition was so demanding it would probably never be fulfilled in reality.[35] Marxist-Leninist theory then tried in earnest to create the utopian unity of popular will and the rule of reason, by simply declaring the people to be the proletariat and the proletariat to be the vehicle of mankind's reasonable destiny. The party carried out the dictates of reason and furnished them with the sovereign power of the people.

"*We* are the people"—this cry from the crowd that was physically present was therefore the revolt of "the people" in the larger sense, the revolt of a multitude of individuals against an enforced identity as a unit whose empirical will was made totally subject to a historical process as interpreted by the Communist Party. The amazement of the world at the "peaceful revolutions" in Czechoslovakia and the German Democratic Republic in the autumn of 1989 surely stems from the fact that the people did not "take up arms," as we are used to hearing, but brought down their heavily armed governments by means of civil disobedience instead. The peaceful character of these revolutions finds its inner logic in the fact that they were uprisings not of an "I" forged by smelting individuals into a single united subject, but of a "we"—an assembly of citizens in which each is individually responsible for his actions. It is then no accident that their demands involved fundamental human rights and not political power, which was literally available for the taking for several weeks in the GDR yet was never seized by any of the revolutionary groups, either "in the name of the people" or in the name of any other collective idea.

Instead, their political aims were directed at creating a new constitution, and it is here that, paradoxically, we can recognize the revolutionary core at the heart of this political revolt. For the significance of this political act, which was intuitively grasped rather than strategically conceived, lies in its rejection of the concept of a people existing prior to and above the constitution, which as a *pouvoir constituant*[36] has the quasi-natural right to exercise a *potestas absoluta* [absolute power], to create any kind of new order it desires, and to impose its will on society. This represents a break with a fundamental assumption of the continental European tradition about the state and the correction of a common interpretation of the connection between revolution and progress as well. The axiom thus placed in question is the doctrine of the unity and indivisibility of sovereignty as developed by Jean Bodin to support the superior power of the state, sovereignty which is transferred unaltered to the nation and then directly to the people. As Title 3, Article 1 of the French Constitution of 1791 declares: "Sovereignty is one, indivisible, inalienable, and imprescriptible: it belongs to the nation."[37] If sovereignty is one, then the possessor of it must also represent a single unity, and thus nations and, after the elimination of the monarchy, the people must be regarded as a single subject that acts like a single person. Phrases such as "the people that rises up against its masters," "the power of the people," or *"pouvoir constituant"* reflect this notion of a homogeneous unit in a variety of ways, and in the spontaneous mass actions of the French Revolution these metaphors did in fact have a certain correspondence to reality. In terms of constitutional theory, the construct of the *pouvoir constituant* had the important function for the French revolutionaries in 1789 of constituting the nation as a subject outside of all constitutional limitations, in order to give the National Assembly an unchallengeable legitimation as it drafted a constitution. If the nation exists prior to the constitution, its unity is not constituted by it. The same argument applies to the people. Thus strictly speaking popular sovereignty was not a legal title created by the constitution either, but a fact antecedent to all law. The revolution was thus justified in terms of the theory of the state, if not legally. Thomas Hobbes had anticipated the antirevolutionary answer to the argument almost 150 years earlier:

> We must consider, first of all, what a multitude of men, gathering themselves of their own free wills into society, is; namely, that it is not any one body, but many men, whereof each one hath his own will and his peculiar judgment concerning all things that may be proposed. . . . Neither must we ascribe any action to the multitude, as its own; but if all or more of them do agree, it will not be an action, but as many actions as men. For although in some great sedition, it is commonly said, that the people of that city have taken up arms; yet it is true of those only who are in arms, or who consent to them. For the city, which is one person, cannot take up arms against itself.[38]

Before the multitude is unified in society it does not constitute a single entity, and after its political unification it does not have the right to revolt, according to Hobbes. With his concept of the *pouvoir constituant*, Sieyès had constructed an entity antecedent to all law, but this created a new problem: He had to find reasons why it was then necessary to subject the preexisting political entity of the *pouvoir constituant* to a constitution and transform it into *pouvoirs constitués* [constituted power]. In the revolutions that followed the French pattern the battle always raged between those who wanted to perpetuate the immediate sovereignty of the popular will and those who, after having brought down the old order and established the revolutionary elite, wanted to have the popular will mediated as soon as possible through the channels of a constitution.[39] They had in common a tacit assumption that a constitution would muzzle the people and limit popular sovereignty—a result feared by the one side and desired by the other. Since constitutions put an end to revolution and revolutions are by definition "progressive" (because—in contrast to resistance—they are not directed at the restoration of an old order but the establishment of a new one), the notion can easily arise that a *pouvoir constituant* limited by no constitution is inherently progressive and that its transformation into a *pouvoir constitué* represents an impediment to progress, so to speak. Here, too, a constitution, which unavoidably splits the unified popular will among various institutions in even the most radical versions, appears as an impediment to and a limitation of original popular unity and direct popular sovereignty. Socialist constitutional theory has always understood the term "people" in the narrower sense described above as a single subject able to feel and act as a unit—just as the French National Assembly understood "nation" in 1789. However, neither socialist theory nor the National Assembly ever allowed itself to be swayed by the seductive populist equation "direct popular power = progressiveness." Instead, as we have seen, socialist constitutional theory projected the idea of historical progress onto the people in the exclusive sense, that is, the proletariat. This did not prevent it from making certain practical concessions to expressions of the people's will in the form of plebiscites;[40] at no time, however, did it abandon the principle that a form of rule is democratic not because the people rule themselves but because and to the extent that the people embody progress and thus represent an idea. Socialist theory had no major difficulty in labeling popular uprisings—such as those in the GDR in 1953, in Hungary and Poland in 1956, and in Czechoslovakia in 1968—as counterrevolutionary. This occurred not because these revolts lacked broad popular support—socialists had recognized far smaller movements as truly revolutionary—but because they ran counter to the grand design of historical progress as conceived by the party. (It is significant in this context that a decisive step in ending Communist-Party rule in Hungary appeared on the surface to be merely the solution of a semantic problem: Not until the communist leadership admitted in May 1989 that the events of the autumn of 1956 were not a counterrevolution but a popular uprising was the democratic revolution irrevocably on the road to victory.) In the democratic revolutions of 1989 "the people" appear in a third sense: not as a unified *pouvoir constituant*, nor as a *pouvoir constitué*, but in the paradoxical form of a totality which does not absorb the multiplicity of single individuals and their diversity in a unified political will. In the two following chapters our aim will be to reach a better understanding of these revolutions and their puzzling character.

Notes

1. For more on how these "asymmetrical opposites" function see R. Koselleck, "Zur historisch-politischen Semantik asymmetrischer Gegenbegriffe," in R. Koselleck, ed., *Vergangene Zukunft*, 211ff.
2. P. Kondylis, "Reaktion, Restauration," in Brunner et al., eds., *Geschichtliche Grundbergriffe 5*, 179ff, 200.
3. D. Langewiesche, "'Fortschritt', 'Tradition', und 'Reaktion' nach der französischen Revolution bis zu den Revolutionen von 1848," in J. Schmidt, ed., *Aufklärung und Gegenaufklärung in der europäischen Literatur, Philosophie und Politik von der Antike bis zur Gegenwart* (Darmstadt, 1989), 446ff, 450, 451.
4. K. Freiherr zum Altenstein, "Rigaer Denkschrift 'über die Leitung des Preußischen Staates,'" of 11 September 1807, reprinted in G. Winter, ed., *Die Reorganisation des Preußischen Staates unter Stein und Hardenberg*, Teil 1, Vol. 1 (Leipzig, 1931), 364ff, 388.
5. Ibid., 389–90.
6. Ibid., 404, 406.
7. "Gesetzlicher Fortschritt," in C. von Rotteck and C. Welcker, eds., *Supplemente zur ersten Auflage des Staats-Lexikons oder der Enzyklopädie der Staatswissenschaften*, Vol. 2 (Altona, 1846), 448–49.
8. Ibid., 450.
9. Cited according to Kondylis, "Reaktion, Restauration," 201.
10. Kant, *Die Metaphysik der Sitten*, pars. 43 and 51, Weischedel, cd., *Gesammelte Werke* (Frankfurt, 1977), vol. 8, 429 and 462.
11. See E.-W. Böckenförde, "Geschichtliche Entwicklung und Bedeutungswandel der Verfassung," in *Festschrift für Rudolf Gmür* (Bielefeld, 1983), 7ff; "Verfassungsprobleme und Verfassungsbewegung des 19. Jahrhunderts," in E.-W. Böckenförde, ed., *Staat, Gesellschaft, Freiheit: Studien zur Staatstheorie und zum Verfassungsrecht* (Frankfurt, 1976), 93ff; also Böckenförde, *Der deutsche Typ der konstitutionellen Monarchie*, 112ff.
12. R. Wahl, "Der Vorrang der Verfassung," *Der Staat 20* (1981): 491.
13. Cited according to Grimm, "Verfassung (II)," 871–72.
14. Cited according to ibid., 875–76.
15. For more details on the factions see E. R. Huber, *Deutsche Verfassungsgeschichte seit 1789*, 3rd ed. (Stuttgart, 1988), vol. 2, 613ff.
16. K. Marx, "Contribution to the Critique of Hegel's Philosophy of Law: Introduction," in K. Marx and F. Engels, *Collected Works* (New York, 1975), 3:57.
17. See U. K. Preuss, "Was heißt radikale Demokratie heute?," in Forum für Philosophie Bad Homburg, ed., *Die Ideen von 1789 in der deutschen Rezeption* (Frankfurt, 1989), 37ff, 42ff.
18. Marx, "Contribution to the Critique of Hegel's Philosophy of Law: Intro-

duction," in Marx and Engels, *Collected Works* 3:184.

19. For more on this point see R. Koselleck, "Fortschritt," in Brunner et al., eds., *Geschichtliche Grundbegriffe* 2, 390ff, 397–98.
20. A.-N. d. Condorcet, *Sketch for a Historical Picture of the Progress of the Human Mind* (London, 1955), 173.
21. Koselleck, "Fortschritt," 399–400.
22. Marx, "Contribution to the Critique of Hegel's Philosophy of Law: Introduction," 3:186.
23. A. Przeworski, *Capitalism and Social Democracy* (Cambridge, Eng., 1985), 139.
24. C. Schmitt, *Verfassungslehre*, 4th ed. (Berlin, 1965), 242–43.
25. D. Grimm, "Zwischen Anschluß und Neukonstitution," *Frankfurter Allgemeine Zeitung*, no. 81 (5 April 1990): 35.
26. As an example of both sides of the argument see C. Schmitt, "Legalität und Legitimität" (1932), reprinted in C. Schmitt, *Verfassungsrechtliche Aufsätze aus den Jahren 1924–1954* (Berlin, 1958), 263ff, and the early work of his pupil O. Kirchheimer, "Weimar—und was dann? Analyse einer Verfassung" (1930), reprinted in O. Kirchheimer, *Politik und Verfassung* (Frankfurt, 1964), 9ff.
27. Reprinted in W. Luthardt, ed., *Sozialdemokratische Arbeiterbewegung und Weimarer Republik: Materialien zur gesellschaftlichen Entwicklung 1927–1933*, Vol. 2 (Frankfurt, 1978), 23.
28. E. Fraenkel, "Um die Verfassung," cited according to Luthardt, ibid., 47–48.
29. Ibid., 52.
30. Ibid., 47.
31. See Rödel, Frankenberg, and Dubiel, *Die demokratische Frage* (Frankfurt, 1989), 166ff.
32. Marx, "Contribution to the Critique of Hegel's Philosophy of Law: Introduction," 3:186.
33. See Arendt, *On Revolution*, 88.
34. Schmitt, *Verfassungslehre*, 235.
35. For more on this subject see Preuss, "Was heißt radikale Demokratie heute?"
36. See E.-W. Böckenförde, *Die verfassunggebende Gewalt des Volkes: Ein staatstheoretischer Grenzbegriff* (Munich, 1986); S. Breuer, "Nationalstaat und pouvoir constituant bei Sieyès und Carl Schmitt," *Archiv für Rechts- und Sozialphilosophie* 70 (1984): 495ff.
37. Cited according to the Constitution of 1791 as reproduced in Anderson, ed., *Select Documents Illustrative of the History of France*, 64.
38. T. Hobbes, *Man and Citizen (De Homine and De Cive)*, ed. B. Gert (Indianapolis, 1991), 174–75.
39. For details see Redslob, *Die Staatstheorien der französischen Nationalversammlung*, 151ff; Loewenstein, *Volk und Parlament*, 288ff.
40. See K. V. Beyme, "Demokratie," in *Marxismus im Systemvergleich*, Politik, 1 (Frankfurt and New York, 1973), Col. 157ff.

✧4✧

Constitutional and Social Revolutions

Were the events that brought about the collapse of communist regimes all over Eastern Europe (with the exception of Bulgaria and possibly Rumania) during the summer and autumn of 1989 "democratic revolutions"? What is meant by that term? And can they properly be called revolutions at all? If revolutions are understood to mean fighting in the streets, civil war, bloodshed, revolutionary avant-gardes, and the rhetoric of universal liberation and progress, then none of this took place there (with the partial exception of Rumania).[1] But it would be totally false to see revolutions as consisting exclusively or even typically of these elements. In the Glorious Revolution of 1688 in England, the Puritan revolution of the mid-seventeenth century, and the American Revolution the amount of actual armed conflict was relatively small. The aim of universal liberation also played a relatively small role in all these revolutions compared with the French Revolution.[2] Furthermore they were far less future-oriented, since they were directed toward the restoration of rights that had been violated, and only in the course of events did the need for a new political order emerge. The decisive criterion for defining political and social changes as revolutions is whether they bring down an existing order and its underlying principles and replace them with new principles. Thus the elimination of the monarch's sole sovereignty and the establishment of parliamentary or popular sovereignty in England, America, and France are revolutions, quite independent of the course taken by the events leading up to them. It is equally legitimate to speak of the changes in Poland, Hungary, Czechoslovakia, and the German Democratic Republic as revolutions, for they did more than bring about radical reforms within a system that remained essentially the same: They succeeded in taking power away from the forces in possession of sovereignty.

While it may remain unclear who now exercises sovereignty there, if anyone, it is certainly no longer the "urban and rural laboring population," or "the firm alliance of the working class with ... other sectors of society."[3] We can say this much, at least: In these countries the new political order is based on equal freedom for all citizens, and this is a revolutionary change of no less significance than the transformation of the *ancien régime* into a civil democracy. Those directly involved in these changes frequently characterize the socialist system as the "feudalism of the industrial age"; this makes clear that they were aware of the radical nature of the changes and their implications for the old system, even though they are hesitant—for reasons we will go into later—to use the term "revolution."

Nonetheless, the character of these revolutions is far from clear. First of all, there is no single definition applicable to all revolutions; "the revolution" as such does not exist. The American and French revolutions differed so significantly, for example, that historians have attempted to describe their particular nature with the terms "constitutional revolution" and "social revolution." The Anglo-American revolutions belong to the category of constitutional revolution, while the French Revolution of 1789 and the Russian Revolution of 1917 are regarded as classic examples of social revolution. The essence of a constitutional revolution is seen as "a founding of a radically new government without major transfer of property, without fundamental changes in the social order, without a shift to a completely new ruling class, but with retention of most of the elements of the already existing constitution."[4] Social revolutions, by contrast, are characterized by a fundamental redistribution of wealth, in combination with equally radical changes in the rules for acquiring title to property and wealth. Titles of rank and property rights granted by the old order are generally revoked.

While the view of the American Revolution as purely political and constitutional is not without its problems,[5] we have seen that the French Revolution was a social revolution from the outset. The first French constitution opens, characteristically, with a catalogue of social privileges that the new government has revoked:

> There is no longer nobility, nor peerage, nor hereditary distinctions, nor distinctions of orders, nor feudal régime, nor patrimonial jurisdictions, nor any titles, denominations, or prerogatives derived therefrom, nor any order of chivalry, nor any corporations or decorations which demanded proofs of nobility or that were grounded upon distinctions of birth, nor any superiority other than that of public officials in the exercise of their functions.[6]

With a certain inevitability this social revolution developed its own dynamics and opened up the possibility for the impoverished urban and rural populations to take up the revolutionary cause; it acquired an anticapitalist accent, at least temporarily. However, this did not alter the fact that their leaders acted "primarily in the name of private property and equality before the law"; "the main thrust of this revolution [was] . . . certainly bourgeois and capitalist."[7] Since one can clearly say the same of the American Revolution, the only distinguishing fact between the two would be the feudal and absolutist obstacles in the path of the French Revolution which did not exist in the American case. As important as this circumstance was for the character of each revolution, another element appears to me hardly less significant. The "fundamental alteration of property rights and the social order" is only an external characteristic of social revolutions; behind it lies the theoretical notion and moral impulse to see the fate of the individual as inseparably linked to that of society as a whole. The liberation of the individual thus becomes unthinkable without the simultaneous liberation of society.[8] Rousseau's dictum that in fulfilling his obligations toward society "a man cannot work for others without at the same time working for himself"[9] is equally valid in the converse form: No one can work for himself without working for others. This is less an empirical observation than the establishment of a normative principle of social justice and solidarity, whose recognition led the French Revolution to take a social course. From the perspective of political theology it appears, incidentally, to be no accident that this social revolution took place in a country that was Catholic through and through and where the idea reigned that all the poor will have an equal share in God's grace; the Protestant—especially Calvinist—belief in a personal path to salvation could not gain a foothold there. Max Weber's view is well known that this Protestant view of salvation acted as the driving force behind capitalism and represents a fundamental aspect of American society.[10] This theory offers a further explanation for the purely constitutional character of the American Revolution and its primary concern with institutional guarantees of individual freedom. The specific combination of religious piety and economic interest is nowhere more concisely expressed than in the cartoon which shows two Pilgrims aboard the *Mayflower* and one saying to the other, "Religious freedom is my immediate goal, but my long-range plan is to go into real estate." This does not mean that the American Revolution paid no heed to social solidarity and thus to the moral principles on which society should be based. It is just that, in contrast to the French Revolution and its basic theoretical premises, such solidarity did not find an institutional place in a collective will and the republican virtue which supports it. Rather we must seek it in what Offe refers to as "associative relationships,"[11] in which the social sphere of individuals takes on a local institutional form, so to speak, and for which the social network of clubs, schools, and neighborhoods remains typical in the United States even today.[12]

The distinction between social and constitutional revolutions is certainly helpful in understanding the preconditions, the inner logic, and the dynamics of the political system that emerges from a revolution. A constitution represents the gains of a successful revolution in the form of a new established order; even if its political meaning becomes altered as time passes and its revolutionary origins grow more remote, it still reflects the political hopes, promises, judgments, and fears that governed the founding of that new order and still inform it. To this degree a constitutional revolution surely creates a different social order than a social one. However, this should not cause us to lose sight of the close reciprocal relationship between the two. When the French Estates General declared themselves the National Assembly on 17 June 1789 and the Assembly then "abolished the feudal system" on 11 August, their goal was not to alter the social structure for its own sake or for the enrichment of the bourgeoisie but, rather, to eliminate the social obstacles standing in the way of universal freedom and equality. The social revolution was a precondition of the constitutional revolution, which was the goal of the National Assembly from the outset, namely, to commence with "the common task of the national restoration."[13] As is well known, they began this task with the Declaration of Rights of 26 August, but without the elimination of feudalism there could be neither freedom nor equality, and thus it was necessary for the elimination of feudalism to precede the declaration. Certainly this social upheaval furthered the social, economic, and political interests of the bourgeoisie, but no one doubted that the new order was founded on the fundamental principles of justice and progress (above all in a moral sense). German radical liberals of the *Vormärz* continued this line of argument when they described royal absolutism or the halfhearted early constitutionalism as "stable obstacles to the development of the people founded on the idea of humanity" and—in a reference to France—declared a nation to be enviable "in which the forms of government and institutions take this progress toward improvement into account and even permit themselves to be used as the organs of progress."[14] The reference here not only to forms of government but also to institutions makes it clear that the boundary between purely constitutional and social revolutions is fluid. In a feudal and absolutist society, a revolution fighting for the rights of universal freedom and equality cannot be purely a constitutional revolution; it must of necessity be a social revolution as well, while a society such as that in the American colonies, with no burden in this respect, can limit itself to the "founding of a radically new government."

The distinction between constitutional and social revolutions can lead one astray if their reciprocal context is dissolved and they come to be seen exclusively as opposites. This is what occurs, however, when a social revolution is not seen as a precondition for the achievement of a constitutional revolution—that is, as an act of liberation through which the social obstacles standing in the way of constitutional guarantees of freedom and equality are removed—but rather as a social upheaval justified for its own sake, because it immediately fulfills the constitutional promises of freedom and equality. It was immediately clear to the leaders of the French Revolution that the abolition of the feudal régime—that is, the social revolution—by no means ushered in the rule of freedom and equality. If they went on to proclaim the rights of man and of the citizen and to codify the foundations of government, it was because for them a democratic order, freedom, and equality were not real social conditions that could be created by a revolution but, rather, normative principles, on the basis of which society would need to be reordered again and again. When looked at closely, their demands for human rights can be seen to be directed not primarily at particular and transient social and economic obstacles rendering the exercise of such rights impossible, for these obstacles could be and had to be eliminated by a social revolution. On the contrary: Freedom and equality were eternal basic principles, which must be respected in every just society. They are the yardstick for the future shaping of society and thus for the shaping of the future of society; they are, in a manner of speaking, a moral *perpetuum mobile* [perpetual motion machine] of progress. No society can do without them, and no revolution can render them superfluous, since revolutions can alter actual conditions but not eternal moral principles. And in no case can they anticipate the future. In this view of social revolutions, then, they belong to the prehistory of a society in which freedom, equality, and democracy prevail; once the society is ordered upon these principles, then it begins the never-ending journey toward perfection. And then it is revolution which becomes unnecessary, even illegitimate and criminal:

> Every man is a criminal, not only according to prevailing law, but also in terms of morality, who offends against the existing laws of a state in the field of politics—assuming that this state is based on the principle of freedom, that the forces in power have not violated this principle, and that the existing laws offer to the people and to each individual the possibility to express his opinions, his desires, and his will.[15]

It was Marx who developed the idea that a social revolution renders a constitutional revolution superfluous because the constitutional guarantees are merely an expression of circumstances in society which can and must be overcome by a social revolution.[16] His starting point is clear enough and difficult to challenge: Marx argues that the elimination of feudalism and absolutism and the establishment of freedom and equality for all citizens depend on social preconditions which prevent these principles from being valid for all members of society. And so he recognizes, as cited above, that the bourgeois revolution—the revolution of the bourgeoisie—has liberated the whole of society, "but only provided that the whole of society is in the same situation as this class." Logically he should now have continued his analysis by saying that the establishment of civil and human rights in society does in fact exclude one class from enjoyment of them and that therefore another social revolution must create conditions such that the constitutional promises are actually fulfilled for all members of society. Instead, however, he postulates a logic of the social revolution with his category of the universal class and its claim that by liberating itself it thereby emancipates "all other spheres of society."[17] This social revolution in turn creates social conditions in which no further necessity exists for normative guarantees of freedom and equality, because such conditions reflect a realm of freedom that has already been achieved.

For Marx freedom and equality were not normative principles but, rather, actual conditions waiting to be realized; as long as they are not realized, the unfulfilled wish for their realization expresses itself—necessarily, so to speak— as a demand for rights, which thus takes on the "a representative character," in Ernst Bloch's words, and becomes a "substitute-equivalent" for the unfulfilled social revolution.[18] Once it becomes fulfilled, however, this surrogate has served its function and becomes superfluous. It is, incidentally, Bloch as well who, despite his loyalty to the principles of Marx's philosophy, still insists that "the inventory of theories of natural law that have existed hitherto do not become museum pieces with the approach of the classless society, as positive law does." He then continues, "This sphere [of natural law] is so little abandoned that for a long while, and occasionally more than ever before, it is sensible of and an instruction against all usurpation from above, all reification of the means of power, and all exercise of uncontrolled power."[19] In this passage he no doubt had his own experiences as a former citizen of the GDR in mind, and although he had taken care to include professions of Marxist orthodoxy in the text, he was not allowed to publish there even this cautious and indirect reminder of the normative foundations of the proletarian revolution. His attempts to integrate normative principles into Marxist theory could not prevail against the "steadfast" Marxists who dominated the government. As we have seen, the social revolution is directed not against a "particular wrong"—that is, against the "stable obstacles" preventing the application of universal moral principles—but against "wrong generally";[20] its victory is thus the permanent realization of "right generally" and at the same time a state in which all right is superfluous from then on. For if freedom and equality have already been realized in production relations, they no longer require a normative guarantee as rights. The gains of the political and constitutional revolution are thus superseded by the social revolution. The latter's goal is to eliminate the conditions in which any rights or normative principles are necessary at all. Legal guarantees are promises of a reality which must first be created, not the expression of a lasting principle whose normative surplus forces society to keep examining and improving itself.

As a result, the social revolution is not subject to a normative judgment by this standard. In the American Revolution, but even move in the French Revolution, it was the inalienable rights of man which formed the normative criterion by which the justice of the revolution could be measured. For above all else the revolution was a moral event: a day of judgment for all previous injustice and the establishment of the conditions under which freedom, equality, and the principle of justice could become valid, not superfluous. The morality of the revolution in this case does not consist in abolishing morality for good but in seeing that it becomes law. While Marx also explains that the social revolution "represents the liberation of 'labour', that is the fundamental and natural condition of individual and social life,"[21] characteristically the liberation applies to the abstract concept of labor and not to the moral claim of the working class to exercise their right to freedom in the sphere of work. Their moral outrage against injustice and degradation is thus a strategically useful resource in the class struggle but not in itself a justification of the revolution. Their morality, like all forms of morality before a classless society has been achieved, is a class morality, a "reflection of human relationships as determined by social conditions," that is, "determined by the concrete historical social character of the circumstances which create it."[22] Thus it embodies universal principles only to the degree and in the sense that the proletarian class is a universal class by virtue of deduction from the principles of the philosophy of history. "Justice is but the ideologised, idealised expression of the existing economic relations, now from their conservative, and now from their revolutionary angle";[23] this and many other passages that could be cited here testify to the consistent expulsion or elimination of the moral dimension from social conflicts and the revolution.[24] (Here I assume that a purely strategic and instrumental use of moral arguments in social conflicts does not satisfy the more stringent criteria of moral reasons behind social demands.) The "emancipation of labor," which is pronounced so emphatically to be the emancipation of society, appears as the mechanical enforcement of impersonal laws, and in consequence Marx and Engels make no reference to the "collective experience of society's withholding of legal and moral recognition"[25] of work—let alone making it the basis of a justification of revolution. This would, however, place the social revolution in a moral context instead of a context of the philosophy of history.

Since through this denormatizing of social conflicts Marxism robs itself of the possibility of "anchoring the normative goals of its own project in the same social process that it has constantly in view under the category of 'class struggle,'"[26] the characterization of a revolution as social also becomes separated from the moral connotations of the paired terms "progress/reaction." However, the author of the article "Legal Progress" in Rotteck and Welcker's *Staats-Lexikon* says, "By revolution I understand ... a progression from the principle of subjection or nonfreedom toward freedom." It is a progression on the way to universal moral principles, and therefore the author also asks whether revolution is "*legally* permissible, that is, compatible with the laws of morality."[27] Revolution can be justified only by moral principles, and a revolution is progressive only to the extent that the reasons for it coincide with universal human rights. For Marx the justification for revolution lies not in morality, but in the philosophy of history. The decisive question for him is whether the participants in the revolution are the historically necessary vehicles of progress and reaction, of revolution and counterrevolution; it is only on the basis of the answer to this that their actions and goals can be judged in moral terms. Thus "progressive" and "reactionary" are no longer the attributes of actions carried out in the name of certain moral principles; instead the moral quality of any action follows from its relationship to "progress" or "reaction" as defined by the philosophy of history. Herein lies the peculiar quality of a social revolution that has lost its links to a constitutional revolution. A social revolution is more progressive than a merely constitutional one because it declares morality to be a matter of the prerevolutionary past, while for a constitutional revolution morality does not develop its validity until after the revolution has been successful. Thus the social revolution which "fights for the right of man" was extremely ambiguous in this Marxist version from the beginning. It promised to eliminate injustice and oppression, but it did not promise justice and rights. It promised only "emancipation from the enslaving conditions that make them necessary."[28]

Notes

1. S. Lukes points this out correctly in "Marxism and Morality: Reflections on the Revolutions of 1989," *Ethics and International Affairs* 4 (1990): 19ff.
2. See H.-C. Schröder, "Die amerikanische und die englische Revolution in vergleichender Perspektive," in H.-U. Wehler, ed., *Zweihundert Jahre amerikanische Revolution und moderne Revolutionsforschung* (Göttingen, 1976), 25ff.
3. From Article 2, Paragraphs 1 and 2 of the 1974 Constitution of the German Democratic Republic.
4. H.-C. Schröder, *Die Amerikanische Revolution* (Munich, 1982), 199; see also Schröder, "Die amerikanische und die englische Revolution," 32ff. In both works he cites P. Zagorin's characterization of the English revolution as a "political-constitutional revolution," in *The Court and the Country: The Beginning of the English Revolution* (London, 1969), 198ff, 244; see also Mathiopoulos, *Amerika: Das Experiment des Fortschritts*, 184ff.
5. See Schröder, *Die Amerikanische Revolution*, 197ff, and H. Dippel, *Die Amerikanische Revolution 1763–1787* (Frankfurt, 1985), 112ff.
6. Cited according to Anderson, ed., *Select Documents Illustrative of the History of France*, 61.
7. H. Reinalter, *Die Französische Revolution und Mitteleuropa*, 28.
8. Claus Offe and I have discussed this idea at length elsewhere; see C. Offe and U. K. Preuss, "Democratic Institutions and Moral Resources," in D. Held, ed., *Political Theory Today* (Oxford, 1991).

9. Rousseau, *The Social Contract*, bk. 2, ch. 4, 75.

10. M. Weber, *The Protestant Ethic and the Spirit of Capitalism*, trans. T. Parsons (London and Boston, 1985); see also M. Weber, "Die protestantischen Sekten und der Geist des Kapitalismus," in J. Winckelmann, ed., *Die protestantische Ethik* (Gütersloh, 1981), 1:279ff; for the ensuing scholarly debate on the subject see also volume 2 of the preceding collection.

11. C. Offe, "Bindung, Fessel, Bremse: Die Unübersichtlichkeit von Selbstbeschränkungsformeln," in A. Honneth, ed., *Zwischenbetrachtungen: Im Prozeß der Aufklärung* (Frankfurt, 1989), 755ff.

12. Frankenberg and Rödel, *Von der Volkssouveränität zum Minderheitenschutz*, 246ff.

13. From the "Decreee upon the National Assembly" of 17 June 1789, cited according to Anderson, ed., *Select Documents Illustrative of the History of France*, 2.

14. "Gesetzlicher Fortschritt," in Rotteck and Welcker, eds., *Supplemente zur ersten Auflage des Staats-Lexikons oder der Enzyklopädie der Staatswissenschaften* 2:442.

15. Ibid., 451–52.

16. See also I. Fetscher, "Die Auseinandersetzung mit dem Modellcharakter der Französischen Revolution: Von Marx bis Lenin," in H. Krauß, ed., *Folgen der Französischen Revolution* (Frankfurt, 1989), 39ff.

17. Marx, "Contribution to the Critique of Hegel's Philosophy of Law: Introduction," 186.

18. E. Bloch, *Natural Law and Human Dignity*, trans. D. J. Schmidt (Cambridge, Mass., and London, 1986), 200.

19. Ibid., 203.

20. Marx, "Contribution to the Critique of Hegel's Philosophy of Law: Introduction," 186.

21. First draft of "Civil War in France," in K. Marx and F. Engels, *Collected Works*, 22 (1986), 491.

22. See the article "Moral," in G. Klaus and M. Buhr, eds., *Marxistisch-Leninistisches Wörterbuch der Philosophie* (Reinbek b. Hamburg, 1983), 825.

23. F. Engels, "The Housing Question," in Marx and Engels, *Collected Works* 23 (1988), 381.

24. See B. Moore, *Injustice: The Social Bases of Obedience and Revolt* (White Plains, N.Y., 1978).

25. See A. Honneth, "Kampf und Anerkennung: Ein Theorieprogramm im Anschluß an Hegel und Mead" (manuscript, 1990), 215.

26. Ibid., 216.

27. See the article "Gesetzlicher Fortschritt," 451–52.

28. Lukes, "Marxism and Morality," 27.

✧5✧

The European Revolutions
of 1989

We can now ask whether the upheavals that took place in Eastern Europe were social or constitutional revolutions. Were they counterrevolutions? Or have these distinctions lost all meaning? Observers of the events there could not fail to notice that the rhetoric of progress and collective liberation so typical of modern social revolutions was totally lacking; instead, a desire was, and still is, clearly in evidence "to have a share in the legacy of bourgeois revolutions and the way of life established in highly developed capitalist countries."[1] A high-ranking Hungarian jurist who has played an important role in reorganizing the government in his country remarked that even enthusiastic supporters of these developments avoid the term "revolution," preferring to speak of a "peaceful transition" instead.[2] The latter term was also used in the negotiations of the Hungarian Round Table between members of the opposition and the Communist Party. Some participants even speak of a "restoration," in order to banish all associations with a future-oriented ideology. One hears again and again that the transition cannot be referred to as a revolution, since that word had been so thoroughly abused and discredited by the old regime. The new activists wish, rather, to stress their aim of establishing ties to the legal and constitutional traditions of Western Europe—which they do not over-idealize at all, incidentally. Jürgen Habermas has characterized the process as a "compensatory revolution," one designed to catch up or make up for one previously omitted.

This is not to say that these events were merely repetitions of the political and social upheavals that led to the various kinds of constitutional democracy previously established in the rest of Europe. One need only compare the revolution of November 1918 that established the Weimar Republic in Germany (and appeared no more violent, at least outwardly) with the events in the autumn of 1989 in the GDR to see the obvious differences. The kaiser abdicated on 9 November 1918, and the cabinet asked Friedrich Ebert to "exercise the duties of Chancellor of the Reich." This step represented a "very mild revolution": It was revolutionary because according to the constitution the cabinet was not entitled to name the chancellor, but only mildly so, since Ebert believed himself to be acting as Chancellor of the Reich on the basis of the Reich's constitution. Only a few hours later, however, the complete break with the old constitution[3] was made when the workers' and soldiers' councils of Berlin assembled at the Circus Busch elected a council of People's Commissars to serve as the new government. With this step sovereignty passed to the Berlin workers' and soldiers' councils; it was exercised by the Council of People's Commissars under Ebert's leadership. The first proclamation by the government with a claim to legal validity was made on 12 November 1918 and began: "The government which has resulted from the revolution, whose political leadership consists entirely of Socialists, intends to carry out the Socialist program."[4] This statement is followed by a catalogue of civil rights (freedom of speech, of the press, of association, of assembly, and of religion), an amnesty "for all political crimes," various promises of social reforms and elections for a "constituent assembly"—all in all a clear break with the old political order in terms of political substance, although the outer forms still appear somewhat moderate. The new government emphasizes this break when it declares itself to have "resulted from the revolution." The promise to hold elections for an assembly that would draft a constitution was also revolutionary; the proclamation that these elections would be "equal, secret, direct, general and based on a proportional system, for all men and women aged twenty and above" meant the existing dual sovereignty shared by the monarch and parliament had been abolished in favor of popular sovereignty. The Constituent National Assembly elected on 19 January 1919 thus acted as the sole organ of sovereignty when it passed a law granting it provisional authority to rule the country without consulting the executive arm of the government.[5]

Compared with this constitutionally clear designation of the revolution as the origin of a new legitimacy, the revolution in the GDR is extremely ambiguous. It begins with the fact that no particular day can be named as that on which the revolution began or on which the break with the old order became apparent, no day that clearly qualifies as the holiday of the future.

The list of possible candidates is lengthy: There is 9 September 1989, the day the opposition group New Forum was founded, a group which in mid-October was still being described in an internal memo of the SED (the Communist Party of East Germany) as follows:

> [they] have formed illegal groups in Berlin as well as in the districts of Leipzig, Halle, Gera, Karl-Marx-Stadt, and Frankfurt on the Oder, and in all other districts they have contact persons or addresses. The founders of this "New Forum" are in league with the enemies of socialism. Profiting from real problems and contradictions in our socialist society, they have succeeded in making an impression on not a few citizens of the GDR, including young people, and creating disorder.[6]

Then there is 9 October, the day on which approximately seventy thousand people demonstrated (illegally, of course) on behalf of "democratic reforms" without intervention by the security forces of the GDR. This was also the day on which the SED district leadership announced its willingness to enter into a dialogue with "reform-minded citizens"; from this day on, "the old stereotype that 'calm and collective lethargy reign in the GDR' ceased to apply."[7] Or should it be 4 November, when over half a million people demonstrated "for freedom of the press, of speech, and association"? It could be 8 November, on which ADN, the official news agency of the GDR, released a report that the Ministry of the Interior had recognized the New Forum as a legal group. At the same time the report said members of the group had given assurances "that future activities of the New Forum will not violate the constitution." On 9 November 1989 the Berlin Wall fell; on 10 November, the last day of the tenth congress of the Central Committee of the SED, new members were appointed to the Politburo and Central Committee, and Egon Krenz, the new general secretary of the Communist Party, declared: "We will see that free elections are held, so that the people can send the best candidates to parliament. We are for radical reforms." Hans Modrow was chosen as the new head of government on 13 November; 17 November was the day on which, according to *Neues Deutschland*, the parliament began to carry out its legislative duties without supervision by the party. On 1 December parliament voted to strike from Article 1 of the GDR constitution the sentence limiting leadership of the government to "the working class and its Marxist-Leninist Party"; on 7 December the Round Table met for the first time. On 5 February 1990 representatives of the opposition were admitted to the "government of national responsibility" lead by Hans Modrow, and finally there is 7 March 1990, the day on which parliament amended Articles 9 and 11 of the constitution, permitting the reintroduction of private ownership.

Someone else could no doubt produce quite a different list, but this would not alter the main impression, namely, that the revolution was a continuous process of retreat by the old regime accompanied by mass demonstrations and that no single event of great symbolic significance stands out above all others. Furthermore, as paradoxical as it may sound, the revolution occurred within the limits of the constitution — the *old* constitution. The claim that the GDR constitution of 1968–1974 simply became obsolete as a result of the revolution, so to speak, without ever being formally repealed, was made by West German legal scholars whose views were influenced by the European revolutions of the past two hundred years and who saw this revolution as a collective patricide by the people, who then declared themselves to be the new rulers.[8] In the GDR and the other three Eastern European countries, however, the participants themselves never understood events in these terms. It is characteristic that in none of these countries did the promise of a constitutional assembly play a role in the revolutionary process, either at the beginning or in any other phase. What occurred instead was a process of repeated amendment of the old constitutions according to the prescribed procedures by majorities of the people's deputies elected under the old system. Even the removal of the old elite from office in East Germany took place as provided for by Article 57, Paragraph 2, which stated that elected representatives could be dismissed "by the voters" if they committed gross abuses; it was on this basis that the parliament voted to remove top party functionaries from the government on 17 November 1989. At the same time, however, the "revolutionaries" made no attempts to seize power "in the name of the revolution" or of any group. The Round Tables formed to negotiate in all the Eastern European revolutions understood themselves neither as a "government which has resulted from the revolution" nor as a rival competing for power with the existing government but, rather, as representatives of the unorganized mass of citizens vis-à-vis the power structure. It is indeed astonishing that the leaders of the earliest opposition, who had been severely punished in the past with repressive measures ranging from job discrimination to expulsion from the country or prison sentences and whose lives were in danger at certain critical moments, were now prepared to sit down at a Round Table with the very people who had committed these acts against them, in order to work out a common plan on how to proceed with reform and without claiming power for themselves at any point. Andrew Arato's characterization of these transitions as "self-limiting revolutions" is most apt in this context.[9]

This odd feature becomes understandable, however, when one realizes that the Round Tables saw themselves as representing not a monolithic people in revolt against its masters but, rather, the multiplicity and diversity of all citizens. This understanding of the phrase "we the people" in the plural rather than the classic singular of earlier revolutions means that the sovereignty of the people, the foundation of all democratic rule, can no longer be interpreted as a unified and unlimited *potestas absoluta* in the sense that Abbé Sieyès conceived of the *pouvoir constituant* at the beginning of the democratic era. The association of revolutions with civil war—all too understandable given the experience of past European revolutions—can be explained by the fact that in these revolutions the various classes and groups not only identified themselves with "the people" (in the singular) and claimed its *potestas absoluta*, but also followed the inner logic of this claim by classifying and treating their opponents as enemies, who were not part of "the people" and therefore had to be annihilated. If the idea of the unified nature of a people is lacking and consequently the idea of the unified and absolute nature of its sovereignty, then the essential prerequisite for polarization in terms of friend/enemy so characteristic of previous revolutions will be missing as well. The course of the Eastern European revolutions provides a wealth of examples for this, too, examples that appear quite startling at first glance.

In none of these countries has there been nor will there be, as far as it is possible to predict, anything resembling "political justice."[10] We find such political discrimination and denial of the rights of defeated enemies in all modern revolutions and changes of regime, usually in combination with seizure of the enemy's assets. If one asks the participants why they have rejected all *hors-la-loi* [outside-the-law] declarations in their revolutions, one hears again and again that political or revolutionary justice would only lead to new injustices and that their revolutions were striving to establish and follow democratic principles without compromise. This leads to the peculiar consequence that leaders of the old regime can only be tried and punished for alleged crimes according to the prevailing law at the time their deeds were committed, that is, the law that was created to support and protect the old regime. Seizure of the immense assets of the political parties and mass organizations of the old regime is also proceeding not simply by dispossession but according to democratic principles. If it can be proved that they were not acquired by rightful means, then the assets will be returned to the previous owners. However, this notion that democratic principles are eternal, as it were, and override all legal judgments that may have been passed in the interim can lead to situations almost as brutal as revolutionary dispossessions. If, as is now occurring—no doubt under pressure from the federal German government—all titles of ownership acquired in the GDR after 1945 are to be reexamined for legality and rescinded when they do not meet democratic criteria, this is the logical result of one of the central premises of the revolution: namely, conscious neglect of the fact that every democratic and constitutional state is based on a preconstitutional consensus of political order which must first come to power and create the conditions under which a constitutional order can be established. The Eastern European revolutions are characterized in large part by the absence of this preconstitutional consensus. It thus becomes understandable that on 4 November 1989—the day on which many participants and observers consider the decisive revolutionary breakthrough in the GDR to have occurred—the crowd of several hundred thousand demonstrated in East Berlin for the rights of free speech and assembly as guaranteed by Articles 27 and 28 of the GDR constitution: They were demonstrating not against the existing constitution but against its permanent violation by the old regime; they were acting, that is to say, in full conformity with the constitution, and yet there can be no doubt that what they brought about before, on, and after 4 November was a revolution, since it thoroughly destroyed the foundations of the old political system. History knows many revolutionaries without a revolution,[11] but here we seem to have been witnesses to that most unusual case: a revolution without revolutionaries.

We can perhaps find the key to understanding this paradox in the relationship of revolutions to power. The hesitancy to use the term "revolution," or the addition of the qualifiers "peaceful," "legal," or "constitutional," the contractual conception of the Round Tables, the rejection of political or revolutionary justice in favor of something like a retroactive democratic principle, or, to give a last example, the lack of the new vision of a future society so typical of revolutions—all these characteristics of the revolutions of 1989 are linked by one thing: They reject the intention so typical of earlier European revolutions to impose a homogeneous sovereign "will of the people" on society and to use its power to carry out a particular political program. The democratic principle of self-government is not to be realized through the workings of concentrated political might on social conditions, even though this might has been legitimately obtained in democratic elections; it is, rather, to be brought about by the application of the forces inherent in society to regulate itself. If there is a utopian vision in this, then it is the opposite of a unified collective reason and secularized omnipotence institutionalized in the state; it is the idea of an autonomous civil society and its ability to work on itself by means of logical reasoning processes and the creation of appropriate institutions.[12] If one inquires into the structural conditions of this understanding of politics, then the parallel mentioned above (and frequently cited by Eastern European intellectuals) between the prerevolutionary *ancien régime* in France and the "real socialism" of our day could offer an explanation. Much evidence exists for the conclusion that the Eastern European communist regimes fell victim to a dialectic of politics and morality very similar to that analyzed by Reinhard Koselleck for the absolutism of the late-eighteenth century.[13] The latter had developed a program of shielding the moral and religious inner sphere of the individual from politics, in order to protect the secular peace from the destructive energies of a civil war over religious dogmas. But the separation of morality from politics now set a process in motion in the eighteenth century in which marginal groups excluded from the politics of absolutist society— parts of the aristocracy, wealthy commoners, writers, intellectuals, and middle-class officials—created their own social *loci* for moral criticism of politics and, acting as indirect and apolitical forces, imposed their moral judgments on politics. As Koselleck demonstrates, this proved effective because it was not articulated as explicitly *political* criticism but as moral reasoning, and it was expressed not in the name of the political categories of the citizen or subject but in the name of humanity. Measured by the standards of this moral criticism, political power became morally discredited, transformed bit by bit into an illegitimate rule, into despotism, and then into the defenseless prey of a revolution in the name of humanity.

In the old regimes of "real socialism," the process of their moral undermining began from a contrary point. For them morality was a function of production relations, and to this extent a dualism between politics and morality existed only as an expression of a "bourgeois" consciousness lagging behind real social conditions. However, the effect was no different than in the *ancien régime* of the eighteenth century, namely, the retreat of the marginalized groups excluded from all political influence into an inner sphere of conscience and morality, which in the GDR found an institutional haven in the Lutheran Church, in

Poland in apolitical trade unions, and in Czechoslovakia in the literary and intellectual circles associated with the Charta 77. At a meeting of this group in March 1990, Juri Dienstbier, the foreign minister of Czechoslovakia (and former member of Charta 77), explained that until then politics had consisted solely of manipulation and maintaining power, "but now we can tell the truth and act as our consciences dictate."[14] The dualism of politics without morality and morality without politics could hardly be expressed more succinctly. Since history does not in fact repeat itself, the parallels between the two types of old regime end at the point in the eighteenth century when the Enlightenment began to become politicized, when morality claimed political sovereignty in the name of human progress and finally achieved it in the revolution. The revolutions of 1989 also spoke out for human rights, but in the last two hundred years reason has become reflexive in the course of its self-enlightenment. It identifies itself not with a "reasonable" historical subject, which has a "reasonable" claim to sovereignty, or with a "reasonable" condition of society, which will be created "reasonably" by means of this sovereignty but, rather, with the conditions under which individuals can exercise their human rights. Herein lies the self-limiting character (in Arato's phrase) of the European revolutions of 1989, which one might also call "reflexive." At first glance and in view of the peculiarities mentioned above, they may appear to be apolitical, but this is actually true only if one takes a thoroughly conventional approach and identifies politics with a struggle for exercise of sovereign power and for the degree and direction of its effect on society. I have tried to show that this was not the goal of the peaceful or constitutional revolutions. This does not mean they were apolitical, however, but only that they were based on that self-referential concept of politics which is directed toward creating lasting possibilities for the exercise of human rights. This concept inevitably made the constitution the focus of these revolutions, because a constitution can express, much more clearly than the principle of the unified will of a subject, the political possibilities of a society that had just regained the freedom to experience its diversity.

Of course there is no lack of people who interpret these revolutions as the victory of the Western capitalist system over socialism, not without a certain tone of self-satisfaction,[15] and, indeed, much evidence appears to speak for their view. However, no one but orthodox Leninists would seriously claim that the "bourgeoisie" seized power and effected a counterrevolution in the poverty-stricken, ecologically devastated countries of Eastern Europe, whose infrastructure, social services, and cultural and administrative institutions had all become significantly eroded. Certainly the introduction of capitalism in these countries will lead to the formation of new classes, to new dependencies, inequalities, and social hegemonies. But one could speak of counterrevolution only if we could recognize a linear historical development in which "real socialism" represented a higher and more progressive level of development than all the versions of capitalist democracy existing in the West. In fact, the socialist regimes never ceased claiming that they did, despite their obviously inferior performance in the areas of economic efficiency, individual and national wealth, and environmental protection. If one discounts the no doubt considerable efforts of the party elite to appear legitimate in the eyes of others, then these claims were made not primarily because they would have denied that they were behind in these areas but, rather, because the honest ones among them, at least, were convinced that, while certain social problems had not yet been solved under socialism, only socialism could solve them, whereas capitalism necessarily chained people to the conditions of a limited social rationality. The claim was that socialism embodied a greater measure of social rationality than all capitalist societies because it regarded certain experiences that are central to social life and in part also painful as limitations which in principle can be overcome, while in capitalist societies they are considered necessary and inevitable.[16] A revolution that aims to expand this realm of necessity at the expense of the realm of freedom and to isolate it from the effects of social change would in fact be a counterrevolution from this point of view, since it would lower the level of collective problem-solving capacity that had previously been reached.

It is worth taking a closer look at the different limits assigned to the realms of necessity and freedom in socialist and capitalist countries, since from them we can learn some characteristic forms in which constitutions can realize progress. Following Lukes, I will cite three experiences in which this difference has particular consequences: the experience of particularity, that is, the irreducible diversity of individual moral orientations and perspectives and the related need for peaceful coexistence of differing worldviews and moral principles; the experience of "limited rationality," that is, the insight that humanity by no means sets itself only the problems it can solve;[17] and finally the fact of shortages, that is, the limited availability of physical and social goods.[18] Whereas socialist society claims to deal with these problems through increased production, education, and other means of influencing awareness, capitalist democracies have specialized both their economic and political systems and their cultural institutions to treat these fundamental social facts as inevitable. Paradoxically, however, as Max Weber pointed out, they have not simply accepted these "God-given" limitations of human existence with passive fatalism but have on the contrary been spurred on to that "methodical conduct of life" and restlessness whose consequences the world must now face at the end of the twentieth century. And it is no less paradoxical that the virtuosity with which they have transformed the axiom of the scarcity of resources and the limits of knowledge into the basis of an enormous production of wealth and unparalleled technical progress has now placed capitalist societies in a position to verify the original Marxist claim that humanity only sets itself the problems that it can solve— although in a deeper sense, of course. For one can hardly avoid the impression that they set themselves only those problems for which technical and economic solutions exist.

1. Let us first consider the experiences of normative turmoil in the social world,[19] which Lukes has characterized as "particularity" and "pluralism." In Marxist-Leninist orthodoxy, at least, "progress" means overcoming the moral ambiguity of the modern world through society's revolutionary transformation of itself. As our discussion on the relationship between constitutional and social revolutions has shown, this orthodoxy regards the institutionalization of (universalist) moral principles as a symptom of the deficiencies of socially unemancipated societies.[20] If such a thing as normativity as an element of social mediation exists at all, then its utopia is *"the political and moral unity of the whole of society,"*[21] a shared and homogeneous interpretation of the world that would inevitably result from human emancipation. The notion of political theology mentioned above, namely, that the salvation of the individual can be achieved only in connection with the elimination of the state of sinfulness itself, that is, only through the emancipation of society as a whole, is combined here with the belief in the liberating power of technical and economic conditions. This combination not only made real-socialist societies the model of modern stationary societies but also radicalized, in a dialectical process, the conflict between the objectivity of social necessities and the conscience of the individual in a dialectical movement to such a pitch that these regimes fell victim to precisely what they were trying to repress and suppress at all costs: morality.

If one considers the fate of these old regimes at the end of the eighteenth and twentieth centuries, it is helpful to recall the basic structure of the alternative developmental path followed by modern constitutional states. For the nightmare of a normatively fragmented society is by no means new, at least in Europe. It was present at the birth of the modern territorial institutional state in the form of the century of religious warfare that followed upon the Reformation and found its first solution in the concept of national sovereignty, that highest and undivided secular power, which in the interest of the genuinely political, that is, secular, task of guaranteeing peace and security also claimed the right to determine the religious faith of its subjects.[22] This process of relativization and political neutralization of all questions of religious truth by political sovereignty was given a theoretical foundation by jurists[23] and gradually enabled state authority to cease occupying itself with warring dogmas and questions of morality in general, which now were relegated more and more to the private sphere. This development, prepared for by edicts of toleration, led in the end to the legal institutionalization of individual religious freedom, which in turn formed "one of the important crystalization points ... for the growth of human rights."[24] Indeed, according to the famous theory of Georg Jellinek, it was the origin of all further human rights.[25] This process of taming religious civil war by transforming it into a fundamental, constitutionally guaranteed right to religious freedom is usually treated as one of the success stories of the modern nation-state: It is seen as having kept the self-destructive dynamic of modern society under control by preserving undivided sovereignty, by defeating the attack on politics by particularist social forces and their competing moralities, and by declaring religion a private matter.

However, one can accent this story differently, so that it emphasizes the constitutionalization of religious freedom instead of the role of national sovereignty. It then leads us quite directly to the problem of how society should deal with moral particularism. The wisdom of the path followed by Europe, gained at the price of a great deal of bloodshed, would then be that the constitutional state not only tolerated the splitting of religious faith and the resulting plurality of moral convictions but also made it a positive element of political order in the form of a subjective right to freedom of religion, conscience, and opinion. Room for the moral aspirations of the individual, which were growing increasingly secularized in the course of the eighteenth century, was created in constitutions, in which they established themselves as a direct counterbalance to political power; the public could then exert permanent moral pressure on those in political power to justify their actions.[26] The link to politics led to a search for universalizable moral principles which could function as the hypothetical foundation of a common will.[27] The fact of moral particularism becomes the point of departure for the search for generalizable moral principles for social life, and the guarantee of freedom of opinion is already an element of this search. Thus the constitutional mechanism sets a process in motion of reflexive dealings with a pain-fully experienced limitation of human possibilities, dealings which, while they do not overcome this flaw—namely, moral particularism—do wring some creative potential from it in the form of the powerless power of the political public. This social technique of dealing reflectively with the unavoidable imperfection of human ability to live peacefully to-gether does not remain limited to the realm of the tension-laden rela-tionship between politics and morality. We also find it in solving the economic problem of scarcity as well as in dealing with epistemologi-cal questions of the limits of knowledge. First a few brief remarks on the last-named problem.

2. The history of modern science begins with the recognition that no certain knowledge exists, that is, there is no truth, only probability at best, and that scientific investigation must therefore necessarily go forward in a context of knowledge which is and will remain incomplete. The search for methodologically convincing proofs that a scientific theory is reliably correct, the concept of the experiment, and the idea of scientific progress became the hallmarks of the Scientific Revolution of the seven-teenth century. These ideas gave rise to a new kind of epistemology and organization of science and thus led to a truly   revolutionary achievement:[28] Science accepted the possibility of error as inherent in the discipline—while instituting strict measures for eliminating it as far as possible—and recognized error as a fruitful path to scientific knowledge. A scientific error was no longer regarded as sinful, heretical, or criminal. For by now protective proce-dures had been developed to lessen a potential danger by which the Middle Ages and the early modern period felt threatened: This was the fear that acceptance of error and uncertainty with regard to scientific knowledge would spread to principles of social order and finally lead to civil war—as had occurred with questions of religion and morality. In the seventeenth and eighteenth centuries the political order was kept isolated from episte-mological uncertainty and proneness to error largely by the formation of scientific societies to which only a small elite had access. Freedom of scientific research was not institutionalized and guaranteed as a universal right until the French Declaration of the Rights of Man and of the Citizen of 1789, where it is part of the general right to freedom of opinion contained in Article 11. Condorcet in particular recognized its significance for scientific progress, however. He demanded that no public power have the authority "to prevent the development of new truths and the teaching of theories opposed to its own particular policies or current interests."[29] In this

case, what the constitution achieves is to make a virtue of necessity, in a certain sense, by declaring the inevitable possibility of error as the basis of the social organization of science, rather than authoritatively defining truth. There is an obvious methodological parallel to the social theories analyzed by Albert O. Hirschman,[30] such as Mandeville's trust that "private vices" will be transformed into "public benefits," as well as in Adam Smith's famous "hidden hand" or Hegel's "cunning of reason."

3. This "theoretical model" proved most successful, of course, in the sphere of economics, in the realm of scarcity and the struggle for resources in short supply. Thanks to Hirschman's superb analysis, we can observe here, even more clearly than with religious and moral particularism and the proneness to error of human knowledge, a long and highly contradictory development from the suppression of a form of behavior seen as socially harmful to its constitutionalization. In the economic sphere the process runs from moral disapprobation and suppression of greed to toleration of it and finally to recognition and ultimately legal institutionalization of greed as economic freedom. And here, too, this original deficiency transformed itself not only, as is frequently assumed, into a wonderful incentive to increase material wealth, because the market proved to be quite a reliable mechanism for discovering and punishing incorrect use of scarce resources. "Economic particularism" also became a basic element of what Marx referred to ironically as the "republic of the marketplace" and experienced something like the beginnings of a moral rationalization. For it was without doubt the capitalist market that first led to a reliable and lasting (and also much threatened) institutionalization of the basic elements of freedom and equality, that is, the mutual recognition of individuals as subjects. The economic motives were institutionally linked to moral principles from the beginning, even if these were still undeveloped and highly particularistic in their social effects. It proved highly significant, however, that they were expansive and that their normative universalism forced social relations constantly to correct themselves in the sense of creating real conditions of freedom and equality.

I do not want to be misunderstood: I do not hold with the theory popular in many circles that the economic superiority of capitalism over socialism, which no doubt exists, is traceable to a moral superiority. There are good reasons for the claim, however, that the dynamics of ceaseless technical and economic innovation of the capitalist economy in constitutional democracies is based on a "moral infrastructure," without which it would here, too, quickly have fallen victim to its own self-destructive forces, or would at least had difficulty advancing beyond the level of brutal Manchester capitalism.[31] Capitalism is thus tolerable only in constitutionalized form (and presumably able to survive only in that form as well). There is no such thing as capitalism per se; there is, rather, a number of different capitalisms. Its typology "includes Brazil no less than Sweden; it can be brutal and it can be civilized."[32] Capitalism has no inherent moral quality, and we can discover no natural moral superiority of capitalism over socialism (which, incidentally, if it retains any meaning at all as a term, should also be used in the plural). However, there is something like a moral connectability of capitalism that is expressed in its "ability to be constitutionalized."[33] Based on the principle of individual freedom (in purely negative terms at first), it sets free the possibility for all those ambivalent experiences of people with themselves and their ilk, about which we have been speaking here: greed and the desire to enrich oneself, moral particularism, epistemological uncertainty, proneness to error. In a secularized society, there is no hope of salvation from these limiting conditions of human existence. The only omnipotent power in this world that can serve as a substitute for the redeemer in another world—the *potestas absoluta* of a sovereign people (or a "universal class")—can compel obedience toward some decreed social solidarity, toward a unified moral code and a final truth, but it cannot itself create these virtues and values. Society must tame the destructive energies of that negative individual freedom itself and make them compatible with social life, and thus it is forced into permanent reflection on the conditions of its own good order. Constitutions are highly complex forms of collective self-limitation which institutionalize this process of reflection; self-limitation is thus more than mere external mechanisms to limit power, and it necessarily implies a discussion of those normative principles and the discursive forms of their laborious development which occupy the "vacant seat of power," that is, the power of a now vanished divine or human sovereign.[34] Perhaps the explanation for the fact, which seems astonishing at first sight, that the revolutions of the autumn of 1989, based on demands for freedom of conscience, have ushered in a market economy along with the legacy of the modern constitutional state, is to be found in this context of human imperfection and moral reflection. The market economy is not exactly known for making excessive claims on individual morality, after all. Certainly the primary reason was the experience of the pitiful economic backwardness of "real socialist" societies. However, this experience was also connected with the almost complete annihilation of the moral dimension of political life after morality had been degraded to the status of an ideological reflection of production relations. Could it not be that in the revolutions of 1989 a "cunning of reason" became operative in such a manner as to let the unwilling revolutionaries opt for capitalism and at the same time for the constitutional state because no other economic system requires self-improvement and is thus suitable for combination with a constitution? If this is true, it would be a truly surprising consequence of the rediscovery of the moral basis of politics and a further indication of the unique character of these revolutions.

Notes

1. J. Habermas, *Die nachholende Revolution*, Kleine politische Schriften 7 (Frankfurt, 1990), 180.
2. This information and many of the other facts and assessments of the developments in Poland, Hungary, and the Czech and Slovak Republics were acquired in personal conversations and discussions with legal scholars and political activists who were direct participants in the transition to democratic goverments.
3. For details on this see W. Jellinek, "Revolution und Reichsverfassung: Bericht über die Zeit vom 9. November 1918 bis zum 31. Dezember 1919," *Jahrbuch des öffentlichen Rechts der Gegenwart* 9 (1920): 1ff; H. V. Wedel, *Das Verfahren der demokratischen Verfassunggebung* (Berlin, 1976), 97ff, 132ff, 170ff.
4. *Reichsgesetzblatt*, no. 1553 of 14 November 1918, cited according to Jellinek, "Revolution und Reichsverfassung," 7–8.
5. Ibid., 31.
6. Cited according to P. Henrich, "Vorwort," in Neues Forum Leipzig, ed., *Jetzt oder nie—Demokratie: Leipziger Herbst 1989* (Leipzig, 1989; Munich, 1990), 13.
7. Ibid., 10.
8. For the relationship of revolution to the Weimar Constitution see E. R. Huber, *Die Weimarer Reichsverfassung*, Deutsche Verfassungsgeschichte seit 1789, Vol. 6, (Stuttgart, 1981), 5ff.
9. A. Arato, *Revolution, Civil Society, and Democracy: Paradoxes in the Recent Transition in Eastern Europe* (Ithaca, N.Y., 1990).
10. For more on this see U. K. Preuss, "Politische Justiz im demokratischen Verfassungsstaat," in W. Luthardt and A. Söllner, eds., *Verfassungsstaat, Souveränität, Pluralismus: Otto Kirchheimer zum Gedächtnis* (Opladen, 1989), 129ff.
11. See A. J. P. Taylor, *Revolutions and Revolutionaries* (Oxford, 1981), 111–12.
12. For more on the concept of civil society see J. Cohen and A. Arato, *Civil Society and Political Theory* (Cambridge, Mass., 1992).
13. Koselleck, *Kritik und Krise.*
14. Quoted in the *Frankfurter Allgemeine Zeitung* of 19 March 1990, p. 5.

15. See for example E. K. Scheuch, "Der real verfallende Sozialismus," *Merkur* 6 (1990): 472ff.
16. See Lukes, "Marxism and Morality," 23.
17. H. Dubiel "Linke Trauerarbeit," *Merkur* 6 (1990): 488.
18. On this point see F. Hirsch, *Die sozialen Grenzen des Wachstums* (Reinbek b. Hamburg, 1980).
19. A. Honneth, *Die zerrissene Welt des Sozialen: Sozialphilosophische Aufsätze* (Frankfurt, 1990), especially 182ff.
20. See O. O'Neill, "Politics, Morality, and the Revolutions of 1989," *Proceedings of the Aristotelian Society*, Supplementary Volume (1990): 281ff.
21. See the article "Morality," in Klaus and Buhr, eds., *Marxistisch-Leninistisches Wörterbuch der Philosophie*, 826.
22. See. H. Quaritsch, *Die Grundlagen*, Staat und Souveränität 1 (Frankfurt, 1970), 288ff.
23. See R. Schnur, ed., *Die Rolle der Juristen bei der Entstehung des modernen Staates* (Berlin, 1986).
24. R. Zippelius, "Kommentierung zu Artikel 4 (Drittbearbeitung)," *Bonner Kommentar: Kommentar zum Bonner Grundgesetz* (Heidelberg, 1989).
25. See this thesis and the controversy it unleashed in R. Schnur, ed., *Zur Geschichte der Erklärung der Menschenrechte* (Darmstadt, 1964).
26. J. Habermas, *Strukturwandel der öffentlichkeit*, reprint of the 18th edition (Frankfurt, 1990).
27. J. Habermas, "Ist der Herzschlag der Revolution zum Stillstand gekommen? Volkssouveränität als Verfahren: Ein normativer Begriff der öffentlichkeit," in Forum für Philosophie, Bad Homburg, ed., *Die Ideen von 1789 in der deutschen Rezeption* (Frankfurt, 1989), 7ff.
28. There is an abundant literature on the subject. See for example E. A. Burtt, *The Metaphysical Foundations of Modern Physical Science* (London, 1967); E. Zilsel, *Die sozialen Ursprünge der neuzeitlichen Wissenschaft*, particularly the editor's introduction; R. S. Westfall, *The Construction of Modern Science* (Cambridge, 1977); B. J. Shapiro, *Probability and Certainty in Seventeenth-Century England* (Princeton, N.J., 1983), especially 15ff; S. Shapin and S. Schaffer, *Leviathan and the Air-Pump; Hobbes, Boyle, and the Experiment Life* (Princeton, N.J., 1985).
29. For the French quote see E. Denninger, "Kommentierung von Artikel 5 Abs. 3 (Wissenschaftsfreiheit)," *Kommentar zum Grundgesetz für die Bundesrepublik Deutschland*, Reihe Alternativkommentare, 2nd ed. (Neuwied, 1989), Randnummer 1.
30. A. O. Hirschman, *The Passions and the Interests* (Princeton, N.J., 1977), 17ff.
31. This theory is naturally controversial; for more on it see the illuminating historical analysis by A. O. Hirschman, "Der Streit um die Bewertung der Marktgesellschaft," in A. O. Hirschman, ed., *Entwicklung, Markt, und Moral: Abweichende Betrachtungen* (Munich, 1989), 192ff.
32. J. Elster, "When Communism Dissolves," *London Review of Books*, 25 January 1990, p. 6.
33. C. Offe, "Bindung, Fessel, Bremse," 756.

34. For more on the theory of collective moral learning processes and their connection with the development of the constitutional state see K. Eder, *Geschichte als Lernprozeß? Zur Pathogenese politischer Modernität in Deutschland* (Frankfurt, 1985).

✧6✧

Toward a New Understanding of Constitutions

We must not draw a false conclusion. The significance of channeling religious and moral particularism, the proneness to error of human knowledge, and finally egotism and greed within a constitution by recognizing the basic freedoms of religion, science, economics, property, and the market does not consist in creating self-regulatory spheres which then produce moral universalism, the advance of knowledge, and material wealth at once through the beneficial but mysterious workings of an "invisible hand" or the "cunning of reason." If this were so, then a constitution would truly be the wonder-working document praised so exuberantly at the beginning of the first chapter. But such a marvelous power does not exist, and no constitution can work miracles with the wave of a wand. What it can and in fortunate instances does do is create such institutional conditions as are suited to exert a beneficial pressure on society to rationalize and improve itself. And this occurs—contrary to widespread popular prejudice—not by unleashing the religious, moral, intellectual, and economic energies slumbering within the individual or by restraining political power often seen as inscrutable and demonic but, rather, by providing an operational framework or, more exactly, by creating a state or condition of "being constituted" in the broad sense of "being a group organized on certain principles." A society is constituted when it must constantly confront itself in suitable institutional forms and in normatively directed processes of adjustment, resistance, and self-correction. The meaning of a constitution or "being constituted" becomes clearest if one identifies its opposite. In the heyday of constitutional enthusiasm the state of a society without a constitution was equated with despotism, or at the very least with illegitimate and backward rule. We recall here Thomas Paine's scathing comment that in England everything had a constitution

109

but the nation. "Constitution" belongs to the category of concepts which morally disqualify their opposite and which Koselleck has characterized as "asymmetrical opposites."[1] Today the opposite of "constituted" is the condition of a society which can deal only very imperfectly with its destructive tendencies, its power structure, its social inequalities—in short, its institutionally underdeveloped potential for a successful confrontation of its normative foundations with real conditions. Repression in the political and the psychoanalytic sense are the two alternative strategies that form the opposite of being constituted.

As a rule we perceive a constitution alone as the opposite of a political order of repression. If, as we have seen, progress and a constitution were always seen as necessarily belonging together in the revolutions of the eighteenth century and the constitutional movements of the nineteenth century, then it was because both were constituted through a common element: freedom.[2] Freedom was the essence of a constitution; this is why human and civil rights—rights to enjoy the equal and natural freedom of all people—had such a prominent place in French constitutions of the revolutionary era. The almost automatic linking of the rhetoric of freedom with the idea of progress resulted from the unquestioned assumption that freedom was the royal road to progress, since progress was nothing other than the elimination of unnatural obstacles erected by tyrants whose "loyal follower was superstition." Once again it was Condorcet who expressed most clearly the connection between progress and freedom in the sense of removing obstacles from a path. Referring to revolutionary France, he wrote:

> From that happy land where *freedom* has only recently kindled the torch of genius, the mind of man, released from the leading-strings of its infancy, advances with firm steps towards the *truth*.... We have already seen reason lift her *chains*, shake herself free of some of them.... It remains for us to study the stage in which she finally succeeds in breaking those chains, and when ... she frees herself from them one by one; when at last she can go forward unhindered, and the only *obstacles* in her path are those that are inevitably renewed at every fresh *advance* because they are the necessary consequence of the very constitution of our understanding—of the connection, that is, between our means of discovering the *truth* and the resistance that it offers to our efforts.[3]

In America, where no feudal or absolutist obstacles to progress existed, the relationship between freedom and progress was seen differently, but it was not doubted as such. Freedom was a social fact in this case, and the Constitution had to protect this prelegal state of affairs through an elaborate system of checks and balances. The fact that the U.S. Constitution was ratified at first without a Bill of Rights does not mean that freedom was less valued. On the contrary, the lack of any mention of rights was intended to demonstrate that they were in no way affected by the establishment of a government. Hamilton, for example, asked, "Why . . . should it be said that the liberty of the press shall not be restrained when no power is given by which restrictions may be imposed?"[4] Such a position could not be maintained for long, and so the U.S. Constitution acquired an additional Bill of Rights that was drafted in 1789 and ratified in 1791. It is all the more notable that the sole evocation of individual freedom outside the Bill of Rights (that is, in the original Constitution) appears in express connection with the idea of progress: Article 1, Section 8 gives Congress the power "to promote the progress of science and useful arts, by securing for limited times to authors and inventors the exclusive rights to their respective writings and discoveries." This provision is especially interesting because the founding fathers had here clearly encountered an example of the fact that freedom and progress are not necessarily always in harmony, but can on occasion be in conflict with one another. The rhetoric of pathos always implied that the works of artists, scientists, and inventors were the property of mankind; they represent the inheritance of mankind as a whole in the way we understand the resources of the oceans today, for example, as common property. On the other hand, the no less fundamental principle of freedom, which in America includes holding sacred Locke's doctrine that every individual is entitled to exclusive enjoyment of the fruits of his own labors,[5] would justify excluding humanity from the progress made in science and the arts. This section of the Constitution thus represents a compromise between these equally fundamental but colliding principles. And it is the first hint of a development in which the "invisible hand" is replaced by the visible and ordering hand of political power. It is therefore extremely significant that this article expressly recognizes the possibility that progress is not achieved exclusively in the medium of individual freedom but can also be promoted by governmental authority.

This development gave freedom a rival for the title of "promoter of progress,"[6] namely, political power. In America this competitor remained relatively weak, but in Europe it has continued to play a significant role, particularly under the influence of Social Democratic political theory. But here again it is Marxism that represented most strictly and consistently the alternative to the axiom of "progress through freedom" that had reigned

since the last third of the eighteenth century: "progress through power."
Marxists argued that society must be fundamentally altered before individuals would be truly free to develop their potential and the history of scientific, artistic, and moral progress could begin. And the most effective means for a total revolution of society was to concentrate the power of the whole society in the state. It is well known that socialist states see no problem at all in strong and authoritarian government power, which they exercise with a clear conscience since it is all in the service of progress.

Liberal democrats view state power as an agent of progress with extreme suspicion, and it is for this reason that democratic constitutional theory emphasizes the limits to be placed on government authority. Antiliberal critics such as Carl Schmitt concluded from this that a state that merely limits powers is unimaginable, because it would be politically without substance, and that the political quality of a liberal state therefore tacitly antecedes its constitutional limitations of power (and can overstep them in times of crisis).[7] In his view the unfathomable will of the sovereign people represented this political power, and its support of the constitutional state was only conditional; the people could and must have the final say on the political fate of the society, even if that meant going against the constitution. Marxist theory also regards the latent power of the sovereign—in this case the universal class—as an ever-present adversary of the subtle constitutional mechanisms of checks and balances. Thus many liberals share with their critics on the Right and the Left the view that constitutional limits to power represent a negative and uncreative force, because in the interest of individual freedom they place insurmountable obstacles in the path of every kind of power politics, or they fetter the unfathomable and existential political will of the people, or finally because they function as impediments to the longings of the universal class for liberation and progress. The case of the United States presents an example, however, of precisely what unexpected creative potential lies within this apparently negative aspect of limits to power. One should not forget that the primary goal of the American revolutionaries was not to defeat or limit the power of a state that already existed but, rather, to create a unified power out of thirteen independent states.[8] The powerlessness of the new republic thus represented at least as big a problem as a potential abuse of power by any of its agencies. The problem the constitution faced was, therefore, how to create a powerful federal government without endangering freedom. The solution consisted not in dividing power in order to minimize it but in creating

a system of counterbalancing powers. This was an imaginative application of Montesquieu's idea that power can be limited only by a
countervailing check to power.[9] If the authors of the U.S. Constitution
wanted a vigorous representation of the popular will in the political
institutions of the republic, then an accumulation of power in one
branch or agency was the wrong path, even apart from the possible
danger of opening the door to tyranny. More intuitively than analyti-
cally they recognized the powerlessness of unlimited power,[10] which
can prevent and control, as Tocqueville later argued, but cannot create. "I think," he wrote, "that extreme centralization of government
ultimately enervates society and thus, after a length of time, weakens
the government itself."[11] Sovereignty negates and denies itself when it
systematically destroys the condition of its own existence, namely, information on the object of rule. As society becomes increasingly differentiated, the truth of this observation becomes ever more compelling.
It has the implication for democratic theory that a society in the process of becoming more differentiated is capable of governing itself only
if it can develop the capacity to keep its institutions informed about
the variety of needs and interests present within it. The complemen-
tary modern thought—which Sieyès developed to provide support for
the principle of representation, incidentally—is that the division of labor
and functional differentiation produce an increased number of possibilities for human action—a concept that has been particularly successful in the economic axiom of the advantages of long-term over
short-term investments. If one applies this concept to legal problems,
it emerges that rules which create a separation of powers limit power
only superficially; in fact the separation of powers enables a government to function better, as "specialization enhances sensitivity to a
diversity of society problems."[12] One can see in this a further example
of how a weakness can be creatively transformed into a strength, and
this all the more so as the counteractive forces of a highly specialized
and therefore effective central government and economic or scientific
sphere largely free of political controls is widely regarded as *the* model
of a successful society. For here the goal of socialism appears to have
been achieved by the very means socialists rejected, namely, the institutionalization of progress through individual freedom and the imposi-
tion of constitutional limits on government.

This model has one decisive flaw, however: It is blind to its own dynamics of progress, because in the last analysis it is based on the principle of
distribution and balance of powers (even though this principle is applied

most intelligently). This creates considerable sensitivity to spheres of freedom and the modes of operation of different areas, but it provides no agency through which a society could perceive the processes by which it is "collectively harming itself,"[13] let alone control or reverse them.[14] The thought that constitutions represent a form of self-limitation—through which a society can increase its potential for dealing rationally with itself and particularly with its own self-destructive tendencies—has probably been neglected in the success story of the modern constitutional democracy because in achieving and justifying it all energies have been concentrated on the opposition between freedom and power; both parties began with the shared supposition that its own position would best serve progress—be it technical, economic, scientific, artistic, social, or even moral progress. Social scientists who study how constitutions function, on the other hand, are fond of citing the example of Ulysses, who literally bound himself (to the mast of his ship), but who was thereby freed to listen to the song of the sirens without suffering any harm.[15] By doing so he exercised a kind of paternalism toward himself which can be understood as a preliminary stage of a paradigm of reflexive rationality: Aware of his own weakness and susceptibility, the individual can overcome it by binding himself in advance. One must speak of a preliminary stage here because in this instance we have a morally simple variant of individual self-instrumentalization which does not necessarily include a compulsion on the self to act in a principled fashion.[16]

Societies are not individuals, but they are subject to even greater constraints to reflect, since their social coherence and their form of government will depend in the long run on the moral principles which are meant to guarantee the fairness and justice of their political order. As long as freedom was a moral principle in itself, the progress it promoted was also a moral fact; furthermore the constitutional rights, procedures, and institutions protecting freedom had this moral foundation. But the restrictions and obligations imposed by the modern welfare state on economic freedom in the interest of social justice no longer tend to be regarded by the liberal-democratic legal order as an expression of the moral implications of freedom; they have the status of limitations on freedom, which have come under increasing pressure as a view of freedom largely robbed of all norms demands to know why these limitations are justified. In economic terms they are not infrequently regarded as unproductive social encumbrances on a morally neutral capitalistic production of wealth. In the meantime this process of disassociating freedom from morality has advanced so far that it can borrow its rhetoric from the clichés of popular descriptions of capitalism. "Deregulation, liquification, and facilitation of transactions in product, finance, and labor markets, increased flexibility, tax breaks, and liberalization"[17] are the phrases which are more or less consciously always understood as phrases of progress. However, progress is no longer driven by moral rhetoric but by the naked fear of becoming unable to compete in world markets.

The task today is thus for freedom and progress to regain their moral dimension. Without it we must live with the latent danger that constitutional democracies will be defeated by the destructive and regressive dynamics of capitalist markets. I believe that the other opposite of a constitution—repression in the psychological sense—must become the focus of our interest. The answer to it lies in a concept that I would like to call "morally reflexive constitutionalism." Its necessity follows from the destructive potential of capitalist constitutional states that they themselves have created, a potential which cannot be "constituted" through either the artistic constitutional architecture of checks and balances or the arrangements of a welfare-state limitation of freedom, much less a socialist revolution with its mixture of state property, party dictatorship, and enforced ideology. When I spoke above of the "moral connectability" of capitalist constitutional states, it should first of all be recognized that, in the welfare-state mass democracy, they have found a solution to the "social question" that is respectable, although it is neither above all criticism[18] nor guaranteed to be permanent.[19] In the meantime, however, advanced capitalist democracies see themselves faced with challenges that will put this moral connectability to a new and possibly more difficult test.

As far as I know, all serious prognostications are in agreement that for these societies the increasingly decisive contradictions and conflicts of the future will not be sufficiently grasped either in the terms of traditional liberalism, "the individual versus the state," or in the social and economic categories of class conflict and the social question.[20] These conflicts will include the relationship of man to nature, to his own technology, the globalization of man-made risks, the relationship between living generations to one another as well as to coming generations, the relationship between the two sexes, between various ethnic groups, and so on. The list could no doubt be even longer. It is difficult to recognize a common positive attribute in these conflicts, but there is a negative one: None of these relationship problems can be solved with the characteristic and successful means of the modern constitutional state, namely, power, law, and money. But even apart from these "macroproblems"—which one could assume have always preceded constitutional questions, in the form of tradition, culture, or morality—we cannot fail to see that "complex societies and their constituent parts exhibit a distinct functional need for responsible and ethical mass orientations," which can neither be compensated for by an "ethic of responsibility on the part of elites and experts" nor be satisfied by falling back on the rountinized, everyday moral orientations of the "ordinary citizen."[21] The examples given by Offe—such as behavior related to rearing children; health, consumption, and traffic; or behavior toward foreigners or the opposite sex—certainly do not describe new types of social situation, and I am also not sure whether his rather sweeping claim is accurate that reconciling them with society is possible "only by developing a civilized sense of community that is both insightful and prudent, both abstract and characterized by solidarity." This might underestimate the flexibility—including the moral flexibility— of our modern and individualized society. It should be mentioned in addition that not all decisions in the areas listed need always be dictated by moral principles in order to be compatible with social life. But apart from this possible exaggeration, his theory does in fact expose a new problem, namely, that an increasing number of social conflicts and situations have acquired moral relevance to the extent that the participants can arrive at a "reasonable" solution (that is, one that serves their own well-understood interests) only by following principles "which rational persons concerned to advance their interests would accept in [an initial] position of equality to settle the basic terms of their association."[22] Offe similarly declares that the only person who is acting responsibly is the one who "methodically assumes, with regard to his own acts, the simultaneous perspective of the expert, a generalized other, and his own self in the *futurum exactum* and in this way validates the criteria for action with regard to the matter, society, and time."[23] I, too, believe that a number of the problems of advanced capitalist constitutional states have acquired such a complicated structure that they can be productively tackled (although not always solved) only by recalling the *procedures of their treatment.*

If we take a closer look at the decision-making situations and conflicts that dominate our political life, it is striking that in increasing measure they have to do with questions of knowledge, with its empirical foundation, its uncertainty, its reliability (especially as a basis for prognostications), with the methods of acquiring it, explaining it, evaluating it, and devaluing it. In many areas of politics—including government budgets, health care reform, Social Security reform, and environmental regulations, to name only a few—the opposing sides as a rule are at loggerheads not over differing political options but over the "correct" interpretation of data, the underlying causes, and the predictable effects of a given measure. Of course traditional politics had to deal with uncertainties resulting from incomplete knowledge before, but in the past they had (as they still do in part today) the status of marginal factors, since the harmful consequences of errors were limited, at least in peacetime, and were accepted as unavoidable. To the degree that advanced industrial societies rest on a knowledge-based infrastructure and technologies founded on knowledge and information determine broad areas of social life, however, the status of knowledge is altered: It becomes a significant medium for influencing the direction in which society will move and in the near future will presumably challenge the central role traditionally played by power.[24] In contrast to power, however, scientific knowledge—which is essentially what we are talking about—is directed toward the future and exploration of the unknown, and to this degree it is the strongest force driving social change. It sets in motion a process in which advanced societies must constantly "react to changes within themselves and . . . thereby change again."[25] This institutionalized process of change is closely connected to the specific "risks of modernization" for which Beck has coined the term "risk society." The process of subjecting more and more of nature to man's will (which is based on an immense increase in scientific and technological knowledge) is not only straining the environment to its limits but also creating new possibilities for future damage—new risks—which must be recognized and prevented if possible by the acquisition of still more knowledge.[26] Beck has characterized the change from the "logic of the production of wealth" to the "logic of the production of risks" with the phrase "poverty is hierarchical, smog is democratic."[27] By this he means that the experience of "collective infliction of self-damage" so characteristic of the "risk society" is not limited to a particular class or group, and that individuals find themselves in something like Rawls's "initial position of equality" and behind a "veil of ignorance," where neither their social status, their education, nor their income gives a clear indication of which principles they can consider proper and just as "rational persons concerned to advance their interests." The likelihood now seems about equal for everyone that his or her health and well-being will be affected by harmful additives in food, air and water pollution, ionizing rays, genetically manipulated organisms, or the malfunction of complex technical installations.

When we speak of "risk" or "danger," however, we are speaking not of actual but only of possible damage—a risk is a *judgment* about the *probability* of damage in the future. Scientific and technological knowledge has always been problematic since research became based on the possibility and acceptability of error rather than on the certainty of truth. But its status in society was unchallenged after God was dethroned and science advanced to the position of objective *pouvoir neutre* [neutral power] and unchallengeable highest authority. Today we are experiencing the erosion of this last remaining guarantor of certainty and the sense of security it gave us.[28] Our ability to manipulate nature has created a previously unimaginable potential for destruction that would make Condorcet's optimism with regard to scientific progress look positively irresponsible today. Every new expansion of our knowledge simultaneously gives rise to new and dark zones of the unknown and a frantic desire to learn even more. Science is encountering the problem of its own responsibility, that is, the question of how much is known and how far science should go in the search for further knowledge. This question cannot be answered on the basis of scientific criteria alone. And it is equally impossible to prescribe political guidelines for scientific research, since—apart from other objections—this would inevitably lead to alliances of political, bureaucratic, and scientific elites which could develop new and highly effective forms of social control. Even if one were prepared to pay this price for scientific progress, we would still not attain a secure order based on scientific certainty, since no consensus exists among scientists themselves about the consequences to be drawn from what is known and what is still unknown. We cannot assume that epistemological uncertainty results simply from a lack of knowledge and can be overcome by acquiring more knowledge; "more research only produces more ignorance," and above all it produces more dissension about how much more research on the unknown can still be tolerated.[29] And finally ethical appeals to individual scientists are bound to fail, since they do not take into account the fact that every scientist can fall back on the excuse that he is only a tiny cog in a vast and complex machine. The suggestion that individuals can or should "take on responsibility for everyone and everything"[30] is naive at best and leads in the worst case to the formation of self-proclaimed moral elites.

Yet a glance at the character of political discussions in the last ten years teaches us that a new arena has opened up in which political battles are waged over scientific progress; one need only think of the controversies over nuclear energy, advances in genetic manipulation, or the constitutionality of new information-storage techniques.[31] The principles, criteria, and rules underlying the processes of acquiring, applying, and interpreting knowledge have been discussed in political and moral terms, with the goal of developing procedures by means of which society can deal with the consequences of the uncertainty of knowledge. These are processes of negotiation about "how we wish to live as members of a certain collective.... Negotiations must be based on the exchange of arguments, and whether or not they lead to *fair* compromises will depend mainly on the procedural framework, which must be judged in moral terms."[32]

The transformation of science and scientific advances into an object of negotiation and compromise must seem strange to a political culture that has expended considerable effort on eliminating religious and political influence on the field of scientific investigation in order to protect its autonomy. This development is an inevitable consequence of the fact that the most advanced industrial societies have become knowledge-based. As I mentioned above in my short sketch of the development of scientific freedom, the shift in the orientation of modern science from fixation on established truth to fallibilism became possible only on the condition that the acquisition not of truth but of probability was isolated from the rest of social life, and from the spheres of politics and religion in particular, so that scientific errors would not plunge societies into discord and turbulence. *Within* the scientific community, errors had the legitimate status of hypotheses that had been proven false.[33] Science was experimental; it was a laboratory allowed to exist under strictly limited artificial conditions, and it found access to other social spheres only in the form of experimentally validated and therefore reliable knowledge. However, the speed with which almost all other spheres of life have been penetrated by science in recent times has broken down these barriers between the artificial world of scientific experiments and "real" life to a considerable degree. Society itself has become a laboratory.[34] To the extent that social life has become knowledge-based, that is, dependent on "secure" knowledge for its functioning, the reliability of such knowledge must also be tested under the real conditions in which it will be applied: "Whether releasing genetically altered bacteria into the environment is ecologically harmful or not, for instance, will never be known until it is tried."[35] A nuclear power plant is such a complex system, linking a large number of components, technical subsystems, processes, and interactions extending to the physical and social environment (for example, air traffic, geological conditions), that its safety can be tested only under the real conditions of its actual operation, testing which in turn gives rise to new knowledge. For large-scale technical installations, every system is in some way unique; the more complex the system, the less its operating conditions will resemble those of any other system. This erosion of the barriers between the acquisition of new scientific knowledge and real life in society means that society can no longer enjoy the blessings of experimentally proven, that is, "reliable" knowledge alone, but is now burdened with the uncertainties, errors, and risks of science. Scientific activity thus ceases to be distinct from other forms of social activity, be they economic, political, or legal.

These also contain the possibility of error, of course, and could never be tested in a laboratory first. Is not all life an experiment, in fact, since individually and collectively we are all inevitably exposed to the consequences of our imperfections and capacity for error? Why should science have a special status, and why did it have a special status? One could provide a long answer to this question, which would have to delve extensively into the relationship between social order and its basis of knowledge. I will limit myself here to a very simple yet to my mind sufficient answer. Science could make such triumphant progress only because it was freed from the responsibility for and the need to reflect on its social consequences. One can speak of "scientific freedom" only when a scientist's error is neither punished as a sin or crime nor otherwise penalized, such as by payment of damages. And society can permit science this luxury only as long as it is protected from the deleterious consequences of possible scientific errors by institutional boundaries between science and society. These institutional boundaries consist in the main of mechanisms within the scientific community for distinguishing between the true, probable, and false, that is, in criteria specific to the particular discipline.

All three sources of human knowledge—experience, theory, and experimentation—have given rise, in the course of their historical development, to a second order of thinking, reflexivity, which can reflect on the reliability and truth of knowledge of the first order.[36] Reflexivity is of particular importance for experiments, however, because it is only in connection with experimental thinking and activity that it has become a driving force of progress in acquiring new knowledge. Experiments place "the future hypothetically at our disposal and [make] expectation problematic. It aims at confirming not that experiences remain constant as circumstances change, but that the area of exceptional and even monstrous events is governed by predictable laws."[37]

Experiments are "conscious and rationally assimilated experiences about how experiences can be forced to happen"; the experience that human beings have experiences becomes the point of departure for "strategies ... which make it possible to experience what has not been previously experienced."[38] Thus reflexivity becomes a ceaseless driving force to understand reality as a systematically exploitable source of knowledge and a point of departure for *new* experiences. To the extent to which experiences are no longer "forced to happen" under the artificial, controlled, and repeatable conditions of the isolated scientific laboratory but, rather, in a complex and uniquely nonrepeatable reality, reflexivity solely within the bounds of science itself is no longer sufficient to protect society from science's errors. This is not primarily because scientists are not in a position—at least theoretically—to consider the reliability of knowledge with regard to even the most complicated experiments. (Every panel of experts that confirms the operational safety of a nuclear power plant in the name of science presumes it is able to do just that.) The reason for the insufficiency of purely internal scientific reflexivity lies, rather, in the fact that experimenting in and with society poses grave moral questions, for in such experiments the subjects acquire the status of a means for acquiring information and knowledge; they become objects. The moral implications of producing knowledge through experimentation has even caught up with classic laboratory experiments, as the current discussion about the ethics of animal experiments shows. For the time being only a minority of people may feel affected. In practical terms, however, we have all become guinea pigs today wherever the reliability of the knowledge on which a new technology is based can be proven only under real-life conditions.[39]

The conditions under which this may be permitted to happen, the extent to which and in pursuit of which goals it may happen, cannot be determined according to precise and unvarying criteria. But in any event the "experimental situation" and its interpretation no longer lie exclusively within the realm of science. "It is the product of discussion and negotiation among participants who perceive and act according to different cognitive and evaluative criteria."[40] The development of knowledge-based civilization has driven the moral implications of acquiring knowledge through experiments out of itself, beyond the ability of second order thinking to keep up with it. Obviously this cannot be corrected by appeals to scientific ethics, ethics commissions, or the voluntary efforts of scientists themselves. For the problem is not a lack of ethics in the scientific community but the approaching end of the moral and political neutralization of scientific knowledge itself, which has reigned since the seventeenth century—and thus the end of our ability to take progress for granted, progress that was understood from the beginning to be above all progress in knowledge. The interplay of political power and politically and morally neutral progress is breaking down. The idea that mankind and society are capable of improvement—one of the main stimuli for the political and moral rationalization of political power through political public opinion—is no longer automatically confirmed by progress in knowledge, since the latter's own claim to accuracy has lost its aura of certainty. It has suffered the same fate as that which overtook political power when it had penetrated all spheres of life in the era of absolutism, had finally run up against the conscience of the individual, was subjected to its standards, and finally found its rational origin in the notion of popular sovereignty. Scientific progress is no longer a metaphysical truth either; it must be defended by arguments. We can control it only by becoming aware of its moral implications and creating conditions under which we can deal with it on morally reflexive terms, that is, judging the morality of progress by moral criteria.

This picture would be very incomplete, however, if we contented ourselves with the self-pitying attitude that society is being victimized by a science obsessed with progress and failed to see that each of us is to varying degrees an active participant in this process. The development of a technical and scientific civilization is a particularly striking example of the experience that highly specialized division of labor, the difficulty of calculating the consequences of one action in its interplay with many other actions, and finally the enormous increase in the geographical and temporal scope of these consequences have "led to such a complex society that traditional forms of moral decision making have become inadequate."[41] It is growing increasingly difficult, if not impossible, to make individuals legally responsible for the consequences of actions which as a rule appear reasonable enough from their standpoint but which in combination with many other such actions contribute to "collective self-harm" and an increase in the sum of potential risks. The consequence is that "organized irresponsibility" (Beck) in which calculations made for personal benefit amount to a kind of experiment on society at large. Where everyone is making a small but imperceptible contribution to collective harm, and everyone is thus in some measure responsible, no one person can be singled out as the instigator.[42] Everyone is potentially both a guinea pig and an experimenter at the same time, and it is from the perspective of both roles that the problem of how to distribute responsibility correctly should be seen.

This is a new challenge to the ideal of society's constitution, since what is at stake is nothing less than the development of institutional arrangements through which high-risk activities can be traced to certain parties who are then held responsible for them.[43] Since these activities may affect large areas over long periods of time and also form part of complex larger wholes, they are clear and straightforward in neither a cognitive nor a moral sense. The constitutionalization of responsibility will therefore have to be increasingly limited to creating conditions under which different pragmatic, scientific, and moral perspectives can coexist with one another. A constitution of scientific and technological progress can and must allow for moral reflection on progress, but it cannot point to any universal principles which make it likely that society will reach a consensus on such questions. Human rights also become equivocal in normative terms at the moment when the moral ambiguity of progress becomes apparent. Whether manipulation of the structure of human genes is morally defensible (and should in that case also be legal), for example, can be neither affirmed nor denied with arguments based on the "natural" dignity of man, for what is human nature in the age of gene technology? Morally respectable grounds can be found both for and against such manipulation. If we are to reach a resolution, a compromise, or just the possibility for dissension that does not lead to latent or open civil war, then the discussion of these morally relevant questions must also deal simultaneously with its own presuppositions and its political and social meaning, that is, it must reflect on the conditions of its own existence.[44]

To make this possible is the purpose of a morally reflexive constitutionalism that demystifies the idea of progress but does not deny it altogether. It is more ambitious than previous concepts of a constitution, because it opens up a space for "nontraditional, nontrancendental politics,"[45] in which questions can be discussed and also resolved which cannot be resolved according to the premises of liberal democratic constitutionalism and which are not in need of resolution according to those of socialism, where power and morality are one. But these are questions that *must* be resolved in our present situation, because scientific progress has forced them upon us: namely, questions of moral relevance. Many questions have this status today that would formerly have been dismissed as trivial: whether nuclear power stations should be kept in operation, whether wood from the tropics should be exported to other countries, whether animal experiments should be permitted, whether recycling of bottles should be mandatory, or whether high-speed trains should be constructed. The list could be extended with countless examples from our daily political debates, which would all have one feature in common: Today they all fall under the heading of moral judgments, at least in part.

This is why public political discussion must always reflect on its own political function; otherwise we run the risk of creating a hopeless situation similar to the religious wars of the sixteenth and seventeenth centuries, from which once more only a Leviathan could emerge. The "institutions of public freedom" that make this discussion possible "rest on the shaky ground of the political communication of those who by using them simultaneously interpret and defend them."[46] And who, it should be added, thereby contribute to creating the paradoxical possibility of political unity in dissension. Such a constitution establishes no political center in which a society could recognize its own collective identity; it sees neither the state, the people, nor the nation as potential categories for a politically united will that could then impose itself as a homogenizing force on a diverse society. This is intended neither to trivialize nor to deny the problem of political power; a reflexive understanding of a constitution still requires that processes of power be organized and that parliaments, governments, and courts exist to make binding decisions. But ideally power serves not as an instrument for imposing a specific idea of the correct and progressive course of social development; rather, it should create room and institutions for society to develop its moral and intellectual resources and to use them to force experiences *with itself*, that is, to treat itself as a kind of risky experiment. A constitution that makes this possible would take the idea of progress back to its original roots, to the idea of "the improvement of mankind," to strengthening mankind's moral competence to govern itself.

Of course understanding a constitution in such terms does not require a break with the two-hundred-year-old traditions of the modern constitutional state.[47] On the contrary, this view takes up and carries on the potential contained in the modern state and also in circles of civil society for organizing learning processes.[48] Thus, as I previously mentioned, the translation of the class struggle arising from the social question of the nineteenth century into the institutional forms of the democratic welfare state represents a noteworthy collective advance in learning that has contributed significantly to making capitalism more civilized, although we should not imagine that such an advance is irreversible. However, the task facing us today has become several degrees more difficult. At stake is no longer the redistribution of power and wealth but, rather, the correct distribution of responsibility when no universal criteria exist for deciding how to do it. Thus the principle of "majority rule" has already lost much of its integrative function for the category of conflicts based on intense moral dissension.[49] It will be replaced increasingly by procedures for negotiating moratoria, trial projects, minority rights for "moral communities," public fora to discuss alternative philosophical and moral perspectives, and procedures for negotiating compromise similar to the Round Tables. Their success will depend on whether they can be regarded and used not only—and perhaps not even primarily—as instruments for solving specific conflicts and problems but, rather, as institutional forms of social self-enlightenment, in which differing cognitive and moral perspectives confront one another, options for action are kept open, criteria for judging the reliability of knowledge are developed, and finally—in a kind of "procedural rationality of the second order"[50]—the conditions of this discourse itself are continually reformulated.

Such a constitution of cognitive and moral learning, in which society makes itself an experiment and thus "hypothetically open to change,"[51] will above all have to strengthen the constitution of knowledge compared with the constitution of power. Specific steps in this direction are already discernible. Paradoxically, it was the authors of the constitutional committee appointed by the Round Table of the GDR that departed from the conventional framework of a liberal democratic constitution's limits on power, although the technological level of their society is far lower than in the industrialized West. On the other hand, the omnipresence of surveillance by the *Stasi*, the state security apparatus, had rendered them sensitive to the moral implications of the distribution of knowledge. The foundation of the revolution in citizen's consciences was just as much an expression of resistance to an imposed single truth as it was a search for pluralistic forms of negotiation. It is no accident that the Preamble to this constitution contains the statement that "the citizens of the German Democratic Republic [give] this constitution *to themselves*." The combination of the diversity of all citizens with the reflexive pronoun can be read as a programmatic alternative to the constitution of the Federal Republic, which states: "the German people . . . has enacted this constitution . . . by virtue of its constituent power." According to the Round Table's conception a constitution is not the expression of a homogeneous and authoritative will—*voluntas populi suprema lex* [the supreme law is the will of the people]—but, rather, a compact,[52] in which each citizen promises to recognize all his or her fellow citizens as free and equal beings. It is also no accident that the authors stress the individual and political significance of the distribution of information and knowledge: Protection of the private sphere is closely connected to the right of individuals to personal data and access to files and data banks containing information on them (Article 8). The passage on freedom of opinion specifically establishes the principle of the "diversity of opinion existing in society" as a norm

(Article 15). The passage guaranteeing freedom of scientific research empowers the legislature to "limit the permitted means and methods used in research" and to establish requirements for reporting "research involving high degrees of risk" (Article 19). All of this represents a reaction to the monopoly on information connected to the monopoly on power, to which specific reference is made in Article 4, which states that no one "may be made the object of medical or scientific experiments without his free and express consent." Individuals and groups are guaranteed access to data concerning the environment in which they live (Article 33), and finally "groups which devote themselves to public issues and thereby influence public opinion (citizens' movements) . . . [must be given] access to information relevant to their concerns in the possession of government agencies" (Article 35).

Although these regulations by no means represent revolutionary breakthroughs, they do reflect the character of the "gentle" revolution of which they are part in that they take up tendencies that are already at work everywhere in the constitutional states of the West but that are still struggling for broad recognition. Nonetheless the constitutional revolutions of 1989 were not merely adaptations to the state of political culture already achieved or soon to be achieved by the constitutional state. They were new and creative not only as revolutions, but also in their contribution to our understanding of constitutions. For they have restored to the idea of progress, which informed our modern notion of a constitution in its infancy and whose moral implications have been increasingly lost, a meaning that liberates us from the false utopia of the rule of a subject of historical progress without forcing us to become either postmodern and cynical or moralizing observers as society is degraded to an appendage of technological and economic progress. Surprisingly, we discover the seeds of a reflexive constitutionalism for a society which now finds both itself and progress problematic where we would have expected only backwardness. But these revolutions can remind us that progress is first and foremost a moral idea that makes us aware that "the capacity in human nature for improvement" lies above all in reflection on this capacity. Progress consists in giving this disposition to reflection an institutional radius of action—in the form of a modern constitution.

Notes

1. R. Koselleck, "Zur historisch-politischen Semantik asymmetrischer Gegenbegriffe," in Koselleck, ed., *Vergangene Zukunft: Zur Semantik geschichtlicher Zeiten.*

2. See R. Nisbet, *History of the Idea of Progress* (London, 1980), 179ff.
3. Condorcet, *Sketch for a Historical Picture of the Progress of the Human Mind*, 124–25.
4. *The Federalist Papers*, ed. B. F. Wright (Cambridge, Mass., 1961), no. 84, 535.
5. J. Locke, *Two Treatises of Government*, ed. P. Laslett (Cambridge, Eng., 1988), *Second Treatise*, ch. 5, pars. 27 and 28, 305–7.
6. For more on this and the forms it took (not always convincingly argued, in my view) see Nisbet, *History of the Idea of Progress*, 237ff.
7. Schmitt, *Verfassungslehre*, 200ff.
8. This is correctly pointed out by both Arendt, *On Revolution*, 149ff, and Vorländer, "Forum Americanum—Kontinuität und Legitimität der Vereinigten Staaten von Amerika 1787–1987," *Journal des öffentlichen Rechts der Gegenwart* N.F. 36 (1987): 461.
9. Montesquieu, *The Spirit of the Laws*, bk. 11, sec. 4 (I, 150).
10. For a social science perspective on this point see J. Elster, *Sour Grapes: Studies in the Subversion of Rationality* (Cambridge, Eng., and Paris, 1983), 86ff.
11. A. d. Tocqueville, *Democracy in America* (New York, 1945; reprint c. 1987) 2, bk. 4, ch. 4, 317.
12. Holmes, "Precommitment and the Paradox of Democracy," in Elster and Slagstad, eds., *Constitutionalism and Democracy*, 228.
13. C. Offe, "Bindung, Fessel, Bremse," 742; Offe cites U. Beck, *Risikogesellschaft; Auf dem Weg in eine andere Moderne* (Frankfurt, 1986), 48ff.
14. See D. Grimm, "Die Zukunft der Verfassung," *Staatswissenschaften und Staatspraxis* 1 (1990): 15ff.
15. See. J. Elster, *Ulysses and the Sirens* (Cambridge, Eng., 1984), 36ff; Holmes, "Precommitment and the Paradox of Democracy," 227–28; Offe, "Bindung, Fessel, Bremse," 748ff.
16. This is Offe's position, "Bindung, Fessel, Bremse," 750; he refers to Adorno's criticism of this model for action in T. Adorno, *Negative Dialektik* (Frankfurt, 1966), 292.
17. Offe, "Bindung, Fessel, Bremse," 748.
18. See Rödel, Frankenberg, and Dubiel, *Die demokratische Frage*, 180ff.
19. Elster correctly points this out in "When Communism Dissolves," 6.
20. This is the basic tenor of the works by U. Beck; see *Risikogesellschaft: Auf dem Weg in eine andere Moderne* and *Gegengifte: Die organisierte Unverantwortlichkeit* (Frankfurt, 1988). See also A. Evers and H. Nowotny, *Über den Umgang mit Unsicherheit* (Frankfurt, 1987).
21. Offe, "Bindung, Fessel, Bremse," 758–59. Offe gives numerous examples.
22. J. Rawls, *A Theory of Justice* (Cambridge, Mass., 1971), 118.
23. Offe, "Bindung, Fessel, Bremse," 758.
24. See H. Willke, "Die Steuerungsfunktionen des Staates aus system-theoretischer Sicht. Schritte zur Legitimierung einer wissensbasierten Infrastrktur," in D. Grimm, ed., *Staatsaufgaben* (Baden-Baden, 1994), 685–711.
25. Ibid.
26. See U. K. Preuss, "Risikovorsorge as Staatsaufgabe," in Grimm, ed., *Staatsaufgaben*.
27. Beck, *Risikogesellschaft*, 17, 48.

28. Ibid., 254ff.
29. See M. Douglas and A. Wildavsky, *Risk and Culture: An Essay on the Selection of Technical and Environmental Dangers* (Berkeley, Calif., 1982), 49ff and 63–64.
30. K.-H. Ladeur, "Ethik der Komplexität und gesellschaftliche Institutionen," *Ethik und Sozialwissenschaften* 1 (1990): 76.
31. See A. Rossnagel et al., *Die Verletzlichkeit der "Informationsgesellschaft"* (Opladen, 1989), and *Digitalisierung der Grundrechte? Zur Verfassungs-verträglichkeit der Informations- und Kommunikationstechnik* (Opladen, 1990).
32. J. Habermas, *Strukturwandel der öffentlichkeit,* 18th ed. (Frankfurt, 1990), Foreword.
33. For more on this see W. Krohn and J. Weyer, "Die Gesellschaft als Labor: Die Erzeugung sozialer Risiken durch experimentelle Forschung," *Soziale Welt* (1989): 349ff.
34. This is the convincig theory of Krohn and Weyer, ibid.; see also M. S. Shapo, *A Nation of Guinea Pigs* (New York, 1979), especially 29ff.
35. Krohn and Weyer, "Die Gesellschaft als Labor," 349.
36. Y. Elkana, *Anthropologie der Erkenntnis* (Frankfurt, 1986), 344ff, and Elkana, "Das Experiment als Begriffzweiter Ordnung," *Rechtshistorisches Journal* 7 (1988): 244ff.
37. H. Günter, *Freiheit, Herrschaft, und Geschichte: Semantik der historisch-politischen Welt* (Frankfurt, 1979), 40.
38. Zilsel, *Die sozialen Ursprünge der neuzeitlichen Wissenschaft,* ed. W. Krohn, 13
39. Shapo, *A Nation of Guinea Pigs,* 30ff.
40. Krohn and Weyer, "Die Gesellschaft als Labor," 369.
41. F.-X. Kaufmann, "Leistet Verantwortung, was wir ihr zumuten?," *Ethik und Sozialwissenschaften* 1 (1990): 70ff.
42. See H. Lenk and M. Maring, "Verantwortung und soziale Fallen," *Ethik und Sozialwissenschafte* 1 (1990): 49ff, and the critical discussion of this article that follows.
43. Kaufmann, "Leistet Verantwortung, was wir ihr zumuten?," 71–72.
44. See also T. R. Burns and R. Ueberhorst, *Creative Democracy: Systematic Conflict Resolution and Policy-Making in a World of High Science and Technology* (New York, 1988), especially 89ff and 127ff.
45. See the important essay by Rödel, Frankenberg, and Dubiel, *Die demokratische Frage,* 99ff, 117ff, and 128ff.
46. Habermas, "Ist der Herzschlag der Revolution zum Stillstand gekommen?," 30.
47. As Häberle correctly notes, "1789 als Teil der Geschichte, Gegenwart, und Zukunft des Verfassungsstaates," in H. Krauß, ed., *Folgen der Französischen Revolution,* 83ff.
48. See Eder, *Geschichte als Lernprozeß?,* 357ff.
49. See B. Guggenberger and C. Offe, eds., *Grenzen der Mehrheitsherrschaft* (Opladen, 1987); Burns and Ueberhorst, *Creative Democracy,* 127ff, 131.
50. See Ladeur, "Ethik der Komplexität und gesellschaftliche Institutionen," 76.
51. Günther, *Freiheit, Herrschaft und Geschichte,* 40.
52. See H. Hofmann, "Gebot, Vertrag, Sitte: Die drei Grundfiguren des Rechts-denkens," unpublished manuscript.

❖Index❖